This image shows one of the MIM-104C missile launchers of Patriot PAC-2 air-defence systems of the Hellenic Air Force during an exercise on 31 August 2004. (HAF)

Since 2000, HAF has operated two S-300PMU-1 long-range air-defence systems equipped with 48N6E long-range, surface-to-air missiles. This image shows a 5P85TE missile launcher and the air search radar of the system with a maximum detection range of 300km (186 miles). Since 2016, these systems have been kept on operational readiness and used during military exercises such as Iniochos, the annual multinational aerial combat exercise. (HAF)

Chapter 1
Fighter-Bombers

Phantoms of Andravida: F-4E Phantom II all-weather, multi-role fighter jets
On 29 June 2022, the Greek government officially submitted a Letter of Request (LoR) to the United States for the procurement of 20 Lockheed Martin F-35A Lightning II multi-role fighter jets following a long evaluation and study process. The Hellenic Air Force (HAF) intended to operate the F-35A as a replacement for its ageing fleet of McDonnell Douglas F-4E Phantom IIs. The HAF's 338 Mira (Squadron) currently operates 19 of these 36 F-4Es, which were upgraded under the 'Peace Icarus 2000' programme. They are to remain in service until the delivery of the first batch of F-35A Lightning IIs in 2027.

Four F-4Es with serial number 72-01516–19 came into service on 1 July 1974. They were delivered under the 'Peace Icarus-1' FMS programme 1974, to 339 All-Weather Squadron (MPK) 'Ajax' and 338 Fighter Bomber Squadron (MDV) 'Mars'. Prior to their arrival, in April 1974, half of the pilots from 338 'Mars' Squadron, had begun transition training to the new type. The remaining pilots of the unit flew the F-84F Thunderstreak, which was earmarked to be withdrawn from service.

When the HAF was called upon to defend Cyprus following the Turkish invasion of that Island on 20 July 1974, the 338 MDV's F-4E pilots were not yet fully trained on the aircraft so could not use them, leaving 339 MPK 'Ajax' to deploy 11 of its Phantom IIs to Heraklion Air Base on 21 July. The 338 MDV soon restored its F-84F Thunderstreaks back to service in Souda, Crete, to take part in any war against Turkish Armed Forces in Cyprus. Despite this preparation, the F-84Fs of 338 MDV, like the F-4Es of 339 MPK, never saw combat in Cyprus as the United Nations intervened and stopped a conflict occurring.

However, full delivery of all Phantom IIs ordered for the 338 MDV Squadron, meant the unit could finally retire all its F-84Fs by the end of 1975.

In 1991, the 338 MDV gave Phantom IIs to 337 and 339 MPK. As a replacement for the aircraft it gave to other squadrons, 338 MDV received 28 ex-United States Air Force (USAF) F-4Es, all previously in use by the 110th Tactical Fighter Squadron, 131st Fighter Wing, Missouri Air National Guard (ANG). At least ten of these aircraft were used for spare parts and were put in storage in Andravida and Larissa upon delivery. The other 18 were put into service until 1999. At that point they were swapped with the F-4Es of 337 MPK. All ex-USAF Phantoms now in service with 337 MPK were scheduled to be phased out in 2006, while aircraft in service with 338 MDV and 339 MPK were chosen to undergo a service life extension programme (SLEP) and avionic upgrade programme (AUP).

Germany's Deutsche Aerospace AG (DASA, later EADS) won the tender to carry out the service life extension and avionic upgrade of the fleet and replaced the old AN/APQ-120 radar with the AN/APG-65Y, with its improved beyond-visual-range (BVR) capability, enabling jets to make use of AIM-120A and AIM-120B advanced medium-range, air-to-air missiles (AMRAAM), as well as bringing into service 80 second-hand AIM-7Fs, which had been procured in 1987 and had been delivered between 1988 and 1990. In the early 2000s, all these AIM-7Fs found their way into service with HAF's 337 Mira Squadron.

A US$350 million contract, named Peace Icarus 2000, was signed on 11 August 1997, with deliveries of the first prototypes of upgraded F-4Es to be completed by the end of 2000. The contract was awarded to EADS Germany, Military Aircraft Business Unit (former Daimler Benz Aerospace). The project's first aircraft was 72-1523, nicknamed 'Princess of Andravida'. This aircraft was ferried from

Hellenic Air Force
Guardians of Greece

BABAK TAGHVAEE

AIR FORCES SERIES, VOLUME 8

Front cover image: Despite their age, McDonnell Douglas F-4E Phantom IIs form the backbone of the Hellenic Air Force's strike force. Equipped with AN/APG-65Y radar, these upgraded F-4Es provide all-weather strike capability. In the near future, their role will be taken by Lockheed Martin F-35A Lightning IIs. (Babak Taghvaee)

Title page image: A Rafale EG multirole fighter jet at Tanagra Air Base on 19 January 2022. (Babak Taghvaee)

Contents page image: The Hellenic Navy has six P-3B Orion maritime patrol aircraft based at 353 Naval Cooperation Squadron in Elefsis air base. Among the P-3Bs, only one aircraft (illustrated here) with serial number 152744 has been airworthy since October 2019, while the remaining five are under heavy modernisation. (Faithon Karaiosifides)

Back cover image: The Lockheed Martin F-16D Fighting Falcon Block 52+M is currently in service with 335 Mira at Araxos air base. It is set to be upgraded to F-16 Block 72 Viper standard. (Babak Taghvaee)

Published by Key Books
An imprint of Key Publishing Ltd
PO Box 100
Stamford
Lincs PE9 1XQ

www.keypublishing.com

The right of Babak Taghvaee to be identified as the author of this book has been asserted in accordance with the Copyright, Designs and Patents Act 1988 Sections 77 and 78.

Copyright © Babak Taghvaee, 2023

ISBN 978 1 80282 587 9

All rights reserved. Reproduction in whole or in part in any form whatsoever or by any means is strictly prohibited without the prior permission of the Publisher.

Typeset by SJmagic DESIGN SERVICES, India.

Contents

Introduction 4

Chapter 1   Fighter-Bombers 6

Chapter 2   The Water Bombers 42

Chapter 3   The Transport and Airborne Early Warning and Control Aircraft 55

Chapter 4   Training Aircraft 71

Chapter 5   The Helicopters 84

Introduction

With a rich history dating back to 1911, the Hellenic Air Force with its 37 helicopters and 343 fixed-wing aircraft, including 206 fighter jets, several surveillance drones and surface-to-air missile systems, plays a strategic role in protecting Greece and its allies. Capable of swiftly responding to any threat against Greece, the air force also plays an important role within NATO's structure, particularly in the Mediterranean Sea region.

Currently, the Turkish Air Force poses the greatest threat to Greece. On a weekly basis, Turkish fighter jets violate Greek airspace (Athens FIR) forcing the Hellenic Air Force to repeatedly scramble its F-16Cs, Mirage 2000-5EGs, and Rafale EGs on Quick Reaction Alert duty in Larisa, Limnos, Skyros and Tanagra to confront Turkish aircraft.

In addition to its fighter jets and transport aircraft, the Hellenic Air Force also operates 39 water bombers (fire-fighting aircraft), 28 search and rescue helicopters, two air ambulance aircraft and five air ambulance helicopters, which help combat wildfires and rescue citizens in need. In addition, the force's transport and VIP aircraft have often been used for similar purposes whenever they are available.

This title offers a review of the history and current fate of the aircraft in service in 23 aircraft squadrons and two helicopter squadrons, which together form the eight combat wings and two training wings of the Hellenic Air Force (HAF), as of January 2023.

In addition to aircraft, helicopters and drones, the Hellenic Air Force (HAF) operates various air-defence systems including six battalions of Patriot PAC-2s equipped with MIM-104C surface-to-air missiles in its 350 Guided Missiles Wing. This image shows a complete system including its launchers at NATO Missile Firing Installation (NAMFI) in Crete during a military exercise. (Greek Ministry of Defence)

Greece to Germany and used as a test bed or prototype for the project. It was first flown to the DASA (EADS-M) facility in Manching, near Munich, on 28 April 1999. Soon after completion of the tests of the first prototype, the Hellenic Aerospace Industry (HAI) carried-out SLEP and then AUP of the other F-4Es under a contract worth five million Greek drachma. The project was faced with delays and the modernization of the 34 F-4Es began in 1999 and lasted for five years.

338 Mira, the last Phantom user

While the 339 MPK's primary mission was air defence, the 338 MDV's primary role was air-to-ground and for this purpose, the Squadron received 15 Rafael Litening II EO and targeting pods in 2004 and 2005, which had been ordered in 2000. These pods enabled the F-4E PI2000s to more accurately use their precision-guided weapons such as AGM-65A/B/G Maverick air-to-ground missiles, GBU-12 and GBU-16 PaveWay IIs, and GBU-24 PaveWay IIIs. These pods were also useful for intelligence, surveillance and reconnaissance (ISR) and battle-damage assessment (BDA).

Because of 339 Mira's air-to-air role, the squadron usually had two to four of its F-4E PI2000s on deployment at Santorini (until 2005), Skyros (until 2017) and Limnos (until 2017) for quick reaction alert (QRA) over the Aegean Sea to protect the Athens FIR from the Turkish Air Force's fighter jets, which repeatedly violated Greek air space.

Due to the decline in number of operational F-4Es in the Hellenic Air Force and also the upcoming retirement of the type from service, in 2017 decisions were made to disband 339 MPK leaving 338 Mira (previously known as MDV) as the last Fighter Squadron operating the F-4 Phantom II in the force. In total, the 339 MPK operated 20 F-4E IP2000s from 2002. When the squadron was officially disbanded on 31 October 2017, there had been only eight operation-ready aircraft left in its service. These were absorbed by 338 MDV, increasing the number of its operational aircraft to 18 by the end of 2017.

The end of F-4E operations in 2027

During his visit to the United States in May 2022, Prime Minister Mitsotakis negotiated with the US government, including President Joe Biden, to purchase F-35As. On 30 June 2022, a day after the Greek government agreed to procure the F-35A, Mitsotakis announced that the country had submitted a letter of request to the US government for a squadron of 20 F-35s, with options to buy an additional squadron.

According to Mitsotakis, the Hellenic Air Force should receive its first batch of F-35As in 2027 or 2028. They will replace the F-4Es currently in service with 338 Mira. Until that time, the squadron will continue operating F-4E Phantom IIs.

In addition to the HAF, the air forces of Iran (47), South Korea (16) and Turkey (15) are still operating F-4E Phantom IIs. Greece has 13 of its 19 aircraft operational, while Iran has 31, South Korea has 11 and Turkey has nine.

The Republic of Korea Air Force (ROKAF) and the HAF are going to retire their F-4Es in 2023 and 2027 respectively, while the Iranian and Turkish air forces will continue operating them for longer until a replacement is found.

The violations of Athens air space and the recent threats made by the Turkish government regarding the sovereignty of the Greek Islands has led to a new sales restriction to Turkey. On 14 July 2022, the US House of Representatives approved legislation barring delivery of F-16Vs as well as upgrade kits to Turkey for its existing fleet of F-16C/Ds if the Turkish government would not guarantee their use against Greece. Despite the legislation, in January 2023, the Turkish government started pressuring the US to sell 40 F-16Vs and 80 kits for modernizing old F-16C/Ds to Viper standard, in exchange for not blocking Sweden and Finland's entry into NATO.

This photograph, taken in the early 1980s, shows 01531, one of the F-4E Phantom IIs of HAF's 339 Mira in Aegean blue camouflage similar to that applied to the Mirage F1CGs. (HAF)

The F-4E Phantom IIs in 338 Mira's service are primarily in use for air-to-ground missions thus the pilots routinely practise low-level flights in the mountainous areas of Greece. (Stam Pittas)

01505 is an F-4E Phantom II from 338 Mira Squadron, which was recently retired from service. It can be seen here during its last months of service during exercise Iniochos 2019. (Babak Taghvaee)

This F-4E, serial number 01518, is departing Tanagra Air Base for a post-overhaul functional check flight on 25 June 2019. (Babak Taghvaee)

01528, an F-4E from 338 Mira at Andravida Air Base. It has three external fuel tanks and a CATM-9P Sidewinder air-to-air missile for training purposes. This aircraft was retired from service in 2021. (Babak Taghvaee)

F-4E, 01503, from 338 Mira, is taxiing in Andravida Air Base. (Babak Taghvaee)

F-4E, 01522, from 338 Mira, departs Andravida, April 2021. It is carrying a Litening II targeting pod. (Babak Taghvaee)

01528 is one of the 19 F-4Es currently in service with 338 Mira. (Babak Taghvaee)

HAF is gradually retiring its F-4Es. One of them is 01505, which has been recently withdrawn from service and cannibalized for its parts. (Babak Taghvaee)

This F-4E with serial number 01512 was previously operated by 339 Mira. It was recently retired from service with 338 Mira. (Babak Taghvaee)

Not all the air force's F-4Es have onboard ECM systems, including serial number 71751, which has been out of service since 2018. Here it is seen at Andravida in March 2018. (Babak Taghvaee)

Two F-4Es from 338 Mira fly in formation during exercise Iniochos 2018, at Andravida. They both had Litening II targeting systems. (Babak Taghvaee)

Thirty-five RF-4E Tactical Reconnaissance Aircraft served in the Hellenic Air Force and 71756 was one of the last three airworthy examples. All 35 retired on 5 May 2017. Their role was taken by two DB-110 equipped F-16Cs of HAF's 335 and 340 Squadrons. (Babak Taghvaee)

Hellenic Vipers: F-16C/D multi-role fighter jets

The Hellenic Air Force operates 153 F-16s out of a total of 170 examples procured through Peace Xenia I, II, III and IV foreign military sales programmes with their deliveries between 1989 and 2010. Currently these F-16s are operated by eight fighter squadrons (Mira) in four combat wings (Pterix Mahis) across the country. Compared to other HAF fighter jets, these aircraft have the highest serviceability and combat readiness due to the simplicity of their maintenance, their low cost of maintenance and operation, as well as availability of spare parts.

Their oldest F-16s are more than 30 years old. There are 28 F-16C Block 30s and four F-16D Block 30s, all in service with 330 Mira at 111 PM in Néa Anghialos. Originally, 34 F-16Cs and six F-16Ds were ordered through the 'Peace Xenia I' FMS Programme in 1985, with their delivery between November 1988 and October 1989. Since 2 September 2011, when 346 Mira of 110 PM was disbanded at Larisa, the 330 Mira has been the sole operator of all the old F-16s, which were structurally upgraded through the mid-life 'Falcon-Up' upgrade programme at HAI between 1996 and 1999.

In Nea Anchialos where the 330 Mira 'Keravnos' (Thunderbolt) is now based, two more squadrons operate F-16s. These include 341 Mira 'Arrow' (Velos) and 347 Mira 'Perseus', and together they operate 38 out of a total of 40 F-16C/D Block 50s, which were delivered under the Peace Xenia II FMS programme in 1997 and 1998. Powered by the General Electric F110-GE-129 engine, they had more powerful AN/APG-68V(7) radar compared to the AN/APG-68V(3) of the Block 30s. The new radar was more reliable and had longer range detection against aerial targets. With a more advanced avionic, mission and weapon system, the Block 50s were capable of carrying a wider range of weapons including AGM-88B HARM anti-radiation missiles for Suppression of Enemy Air Defence (SEAD) missions.

In 1994, 52 AGM-88B HARM missiles were procured through a US$27 million contract. Two years later, 84 more AGM-88Bs were procured following a US$90 million deal with delivery of all missiles taking place in 1998. In addition to these, 50 AIM-120B AMRAAM air-to-air missiles were ordered in 1996 with their deliveries taking place in 2000. Wired and modified to use LANTIRN navigation and targeting pods, the Block 50s were capable of employing GBU-12 and GBU-16 Paveway II laser-guided bombs. For this purpose, 24 AN/AAQ-13 navigation pods and 16 AAQ-14 targeting/surveillance pods were ordered for the Peace Xenia II aircraft in 1995, with their deliveries taking place between 1997 and 1999.

The Block 52s

In 2001, the 340 Mira 'Fox' was disbanded and its last airworthy A-7/TA-7Hs were absorbed by 345 MDV Squadron, which was itself disbanded on 20 August 2002. At that point, all of its A-7/TA-7Hs were transferred to Araxos and other air bases to be operated by the 336 Mira Squadron, or to be stored and cannibalized for their parts. A few months later, the 115 Combat Wing became the first recipient of the most advanced variant of F-16 in the service of the HAF, the F-16C/D Block 52+.

On 3 March 2003, the 340 Mira 'Fox' Squadron was brought back into service with F-16 Block 52+s. Next, the 115 PM's 343 Mira 'Star' was also brought back into operation with F-16C/D Block 52+s in Souda Air Base. The Star squadron previously operated F-5A/B fighter jets and their primary purpose was interception and their secondary role was bombing. Each one of these squadrons received 12 F-16Cs and eight F-16Ds.

The Block 52+s were delivered following a US$2.3 billion deal placed in June 2000 for 34 F-16Cs and 16 F-16Ds through the 'Peace Xenia III' FMS programme. In addition to the first 50 aircraft, an extra US$183 million order was placed for ten more aircraft consisting of six F-16Cs and four F-16Ds in 2001 enabling the air force to use them as replacements for its ageing F-4Es of 337 Mira Squadron. Equipped with F100-PW-229 engines and state-of-the-art APG-68(V)9 radars, these aircraft became the most advanced variant of their kind in HAF service. They had capacity to use 2,271 litres (600 gallons) in their external fuel tanks and conformal fuel tanks, enabling the aircraft to reach Cyprus and carry out airstrikes, air support and interdiction missions, if required.

To replace its ageing A-7E, A-7H, TA-7C and TA-7H attack aircraft in service with 335 and 336 Mira, the Hellenic Air Force ordered 30 more F-16 Block 52+s including 12 F-16Ds on 13 December 2005. These were delivered under the Peace Xenia-IV FMS programme, with a total value of US$3.1 billion in 2009 and 2010. The 335 Mira Squadron became the first operator of the most advanced variant of the F-16 in Europe, receiving its first aircraft in 2009 and the last in February 2010. A month later, 335 Mira received its new weapons including JDAMs and JSOWs, the Link-16 and a new recce pod. 335 Mira Squadron retired its A-7Hs beginning 27 March 2007 and its last nine A-7Es were withdrawn from service on 5 November of that year.

The package ordered through the Peace Xenia-IV FMS programme consisted of 30 F100-PW-229 engines and APG-68(V)9 radars, 32 joint helmet-mounted cueing systems (JHMCS), 30 AN/AVS-9 Generation III NVGs, 142 LAU-129/A launchers, 34 Link-16 MIDS-LVTs, Two Link-16 ground stations, ten LANTIRN pods, two recce pods, two recce ground stations, 30 APX-113 advanced IFF systems, 32 AN/ALQ-187s as part of the Advanced Self-Protection Integrated Suite (ASPIS), three spare F100-PW-229 engines, three APG-68(V)9 spare radar sets, four AGM-154C JSOWs, six JDAMs (three BLU-10 and three MK-84 bomb bodies) and four wind-corrected munitions dispensers (WCMD). Forty more AGM-154C Joint Stand-Off Weapons (JSOW) 260 AIM-120C7s, 100 GBU-31 JDAMs and 50 more laser-guided bombs were procured between 2008 and 2011 with delivery taking place between 2009 and 2012.

On 17 October 2014, the LTV A-7 Corsair II was officially withdrawn from service with the HAF during an official ceremony at Araxos Air Base leaving the 336 Mira with no aircraft. The squadron officially resumed its operations, this time with the F-16C/D Block 52Ms beginning 13 July 2015. Two years later and following the disbandment of the 348 Tactical Reconnaissance Squadron, the tactical reconnaissance missions were carried out by the F-16C/D Block 52Ms of the 336 Mira equipped with the Goodrich DB-110 airborne reconnaissance systems.

Modernising F-16 Block 52s

In total, 83 F-16 Block 52+/52Ms are currently being upgraded to F-16V Viper Block 72 standard to remain in service for at least three more decades. Hellenic Aerospace Industries is contracted to carry out modernization of the aircraft jointly with Lockheed Martin.

On 17 October 2017, the US State Department approved the possible sale to the government of Greece to upgrade its air force's 123 F-16 Block 50 and 52+s to Block 70/72 configuration at a cost of US$2,404 billion.

In 2017, the Greek government requested a possible purchase of 125 AN/APG-83 active electronically scanned array (AESA) radars including two spares; 123 modular mission computers (MMCs); 123 LINK-16 multi-functional information distribution system joint tactical radio systems (MIDS-JTRS) with TACtical Air Navigation (TACAN) and Electronic Horizontal Situation Indicator (EHSI) systems, 123 LN260 embedded global navigation systems (EGI)/inertial navigation systems (INS); and 123 improved programmable display generators (iPDGs).

Also included in the proposed sale were up to 123 APX-126 advanced identification friend or foe (AIFF) combined interrogator transponders (CIT); one joint mission planning system (JMPS); one F-16V simulator; the upgrade of two existing simulators; one avionics level test station; secure communications, cryptographic equipment and navigation equipment; the upgrade and integration of the advanced self-protection integrated suite (ASPIS) I to ASPIS II on 26 F-16s; a ground support system, systems integration and test; spares and repair parts, support and test equipment; personnel training and training equipment; publications and technical documentation; US government and contractor engineering, logistical and technical support services; and other related elements of logistics and programme support.

The F-16V's radar, the APG-83, is an active electronically scanned array (AESA) radar that provides multi-mode capability. The APG-83 beam agility enables interleaved air-to-air and air-to-surface operations that can be tailored to meet specific mission requirements. The APG-83 is three to five times more reliable than legacy mechanically scanned APG-68(V)9 radars, which means higher availability rates and lower sustainment costs.

The APG-83 AESA radar of F-16V Block 70/72 provides long-range search and track capability against airborne targets, regardless of their aspect. Multi-target track provides good track quality on at least 20 targets within ±60 degrees of the F-16 nose while continuing to support a designated scan pattern. The air combat mode automatically acquires and tracks the first target detected within the scan volume selected by the pilot. Also, the APG-83 can detect and track fixed and moving ground and sea targets. The high-resolution synthetic aperture mode enables autonomous, all-environment precision targeting. Most of the air-to-air and air-to-surface modes can be interleaved on a scan-to-scan basis providing the pilot with increased situational awareness and operational effectiveness and survivability.

Due to budget limitations, the plan for modernisation of the F-16s was revised and only 83 F-16C/D Block 52+/52Ms were chosen to be upgraded to F-16V level at a cost of US$1.3 billion, which included a 10 to 15 per cent discount. Finally on 20 December 2018, Greece's government approved the programme to upgrade the Block 52s. The first prototype of the HAF's F-16Vs flew in 2021 while delivery of the first two modernized F-16s took place in 2022.

The final value of the contract for modernising 83+1 F-16C/Ds was increased to US$1.45 billion including US$996.8 million for a subcontract with the Lockheed Martin Corp. US$452.2 million will be shared among other companies including Hellenic Aerospace Industries (HAI) Co. All of the 83 aircraft are being modernised in HAI's facility in Tanagra, Greece, with only the prototype sent to Fort Worth, Texas, for testing in 2021.

HAF's fighter force in the 2020s

The HAF has 153 F-16s in service 114 single-seaters and 39 twin-seaters (combat trainer). If categorised by Blocks, 32 are Block 30s, 38 are Block 50s, 53 are Block 52+s and 30 are Block 52Ms (previously known as Block 52+ Advanced). These are in service with eight fighter squadrons in four combat wings. Ready for Quick Reaction Alert (QRA), they are armed with AIM-9Ms or IRIS-Ts and AIM-120C5s or AIM-120C7s.

An Araxos-based Block 52M equipped with a DB-110 pod is always in readiness for tactical reconnaissance missions. In addition, six F-16C/Ds armed with AGM-65Gs or GBU-24s and GBU-31s are standing in QRA for air-to-ground missions in Araxos, Nea Anchialos and Souda. Until 2017, the RF-4E tactical reconnaissance aircraft of HAF's 348 Tactical Reconnaissance Squadron undertook reconnaissance missions from Larissa Air Base. Now this task is carried out by F-16Cs by means of the DB-110 pods.

HAF's F-16 squadrons are 111 Pretix Mahis (PM) or Combat Wing, 330 Mira, which has 28 F-16C-30-CFs, and four F-16D-30-CFs at Néa Anghialos AB; 116 PM's 335 and 336 Mira with a total of 20 F-16C-52+CF Advanced and 10 F-16D-52+CF Advanced at Araxos AB; 110 PM's 337 Mira

This F-16C Block 52+M from 335 Mira Squadron was used as a test bed for Greece's F-16V programme. It is seen on transit flight to Fort Worth, Texas, through Charleroi, Belgium, on 17 February 2021. (Babak Taghvaee)

with 12 F-16C-52+CFs and six F-16D-52+CFs at Larissa; 115 PM's 340 Mira with 12 F-16C-52+CFs and seven F-16D-52+CFs at Souda; 111 PM's 341 Mira with 15 F-16C-50-CFs and three F-16D-50-CFs at Néa Anghialos AB; 115 PM's 343 Mira with 11 F-16C-52+CFs and five F-16D-52+CFs at Souda; and 111 PM's 347 Mira with 16 F-16C-50-CFs and four F-16D-50-CFs at Néa Anghialos AB.

By 2025, the HAF will have almost 30 of its F-16 Block 52+/52Ms upgraded to Viper level, which will enable the air force to retire its F-16C/D Block 30s leaving the F-16C/D Block 50s in Nea Anchialos base as the only F-16s not upgraded in HAF service. The fleet of almost 80 F-16Vs will form the backbone of the HAF's fighter force to counter the Turkish Air Force's F-16s, which by that time will be indigenously modernized by the Turkish Aerospace Industries (TAI) to a level similar to the F-16V.

008 is another F-16C Block 52M from 335 Mira 'Tigris' (Tiger) Squadron based at Araxos Air Base. 335 Mira currently operates 12 F-16C Block 52Ms and four F-16D Block 52Ms. The 008 has no Tiger insignia on the tail, which is why it has often been used by 336 Mira. (US Air Force photo by Senior Airman Tenley Long)

A pair of F-16C Block 52+ multi-role fighter jets from 343 Mira, with serial numbers 500 and 525, can be seen flying over Israel during a joint military exercise with the Israeli Air Force in November 2008. (Hellenic Air Force)

An F-16C Block 52+ from 337 Mira Squadron with serial number 532, can be seen being scrambled armed with a pair of IRIS-T heat-seeking short-range missiles and two AIM-120C AMRAAM radar-guided medium-range air-to-air missiles. (Babak Taghvaee)

An F-16C Block 52+ from 337 Mira Squadron is seen during exercise Iniochos 2019 in Andravida, in April 2019. (Babak Taghvaee)

Serial number 619 is one of six F-16D-52+-CFs from 337 Mira, which have primary air-to-ground missions within the HAF structure. (Babak Taghvaee)

608 is an F-16D Block 52+ (F-16D-52+-CF) From 340 Mira Squadron based at Souda, Crete. The squadron operates 12 F-16C Block 52+s and seven F-16D Block 52+s. (Babak Taghvaee)

F-16C-50R-CF with serial number 053, belongs to 347 Mira Squadron at Néa Anghialos AB. The Squadron operates 16 F-16C Block 50s and four F-16D Block 50s. Starting from the mid-2020s, the Squadron will have its F-16s upgraded. (Babak Taghvaee)

F-16C Block 30 of 330 Mira Squadron with serial number 114. The Squadron operates 20 F-16C Block 30s and four F-16D Block 30s at Néa Anghialos AB. These aircraft will be retired from service by 2030. (Babak Taghvaee)

F-16C-50S-CF of 347 Mira Squadron with serial number 061, is seen with a captive training Maverick missile during the exercise Iniochos 2018 at Andravida AB in March 2018. (Babak Taghvaee)

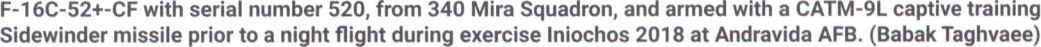

F-16C Block 52M with serial number 012, from 336 Mira Squadron, which operates nine F-16C Block 52Ms and six F-16D Block 52Ms at Araxos Air Base. (Babak Taghvaee)

F-16C-52+-CF with serial number 520, from 340 Mira Squadron, and armed with a CATM-9L captive training Sidewinder missile prior to a night flight during exercise Iniochos 2018 at Andravida AFB. (Babak Taghvaee)

F-16D Block 52+ from 337 Mira Squadron, at Andravida Air Base, during exercise Iniochos 2019 in March 2019. (Babak Taghvaee)

An F-16D-50P-CF with serial number 079, from 348 Mira Squadron, armed with a CATM-9 captive training missile. (Babak Taghvaee)

F-16C-30-CF with serial number 134 is the nearest aircraft here. This is one of the former 346 Mira aircraft, absorbed by 330 Mira, in September 2011. (Babak Taghvaee)

An F-16C Block 52+M with serial number 006 from 336 Mira Squadron, and an F-16C Block 52+ with serial number 535 from 340 Mira Squadron were the second and third F-16s to be upgraded to F-16V standard. They can be seen during the handover ceremony at Tanagra on 12 September 2022. (Greek Ministry of Defence)

F-16C/D Block 52+ multi-role fighter jets replaced A-7E/H and TA-7E/H attack aircraft. 160002 was one of the A-7Es operated by 335 Mira and replaced by F-16 Block 52+Ms. (Hellenic Air Force)

The Mehmetcik Busters: Mirage 2000-5BG/EG multi-role fighter jets

In 1974, fearing US arms embargoes, the Greek socialist government ordered 40 Mirage F1CG fighter interceptors from France. On 4 August 1975, the first two landed in Tanagra Air Base, home of 114 Combat Wing (PM). The first 20 aircraft replaced the old F-102As and TF-102As in service with 342 All-Weather Squadron (MPK) at Tanagra by January 1977. Four months later, in May, 334 MPK Squadron was formed to operate the second batch of 20 Mirage F1CGs from Tanagra.

In 1976, the Mirage F1CG pilots of 342 MPK Squadron achieved full combat readiness and their aircraft, armed with AIM-9J Sidewinder air-to-air missiles, started taking quick reaction alert (QRA) tasks. With the establishment of 135 Combat Group as Skyros Air Detachment on 20 September 1977, the Mirage F1CGs of 334 and 342 MPKs alongside the F-5A Freedom Fighters of other air bases were used as QRA fighter jets to protect Athens FIR and Greek airspace over the Aegean.

In the same year, HAF began deployment of its F-4E Phantom IIs from its 337 and 339 All-Weather Interceptor Fighter Squadrons to Skyros. While the F-4Es, armed with AIM-7E Sparrow and AIM-9J Sidewinder air-to-air missiles and 23mm cannons, were used for beyond-visual-range (BVR) air combat, the Mirage F1CGs, armed with 30mm cannons, were in use for close-range air combat or dogfights against the Turkish Air Force's (THK) F-4Es, F-100Cs and F-104Gs. To increase their combat capabilities, a US$8 million deal was finalized for 300 AIM-9P4 Sidewinder missiles, which were delivered in 1981, and were used by the Mirage F1CGs at Skyros from 1982.

Despite not having BVR air-to-air missiles, the Mirage F1CGs brought air superiority for Greece over the Aegean. With the delivery of F-16 multi-role fighter jets, the Mirage F1CGs no longer had air-superiority.

Two years after Turkey reached a deal to purchase F-16C/Ds from the United States in January 1987, Greece also ordered 40 F-16C/D Block 30s as a replacement for its ageing F-5A/Bs, which were in service as day fighter interceptors. As the Ronald Reagan administration had imposed restrictions on arms sales to Greece, procurement of Mirage 2000 fighter jets from France helped the Greek government to finally convince the US government to sell F-16C/Ds to Greece. The Mirage 2000 was a fourth-generation fighter jet similar to the F-16.

In 1985, Greece purchased 40 Mirage 2000 fighter jets (later 41) to replace the ageing Mirage F1CGs. Having a combined fleet of Franco-American fighter jets (the F-16) was not just a means to survive sanctions but a means for Greece to put pressure on the US to approve its purchase of the 40 requested F-16C/Ds in 1987, with delivery of their first taking place at Fort Worth, Texas on 18 November 1988.

The first two Mirage 2000BGs and two Mirage 2000EGs arrived at Tanagra, Greece, on 27 April 1988 and were delivered to 331 Mira, which had been established nine days earlier. The first HAF Mirage 2000 pilots, who were former Mirage F1 and F-4E pilots, were trained as instructors in France and then in Greece by the French Air Force by the end of 1988. Training of the next generation of Mirage 2000 pilots took place under their instruction and supervision from mid-1989.

HAF also received 360 R.550 Magic-II IR guided short-range air-to-air missiles for use on the aircraft between 1988 and 1992. Later, in 1994, 150 super 530D semi-active radar-guided, medium-range, air-to-air missiles were purchased for the Mirage 2000s with deliveries taking place between 1995 and 1997, bringing BVR capability for the fleet during air combat. Deliveries of the Mirage 2000s were suspended after the 28th aircraft was delivered in October 1989, but resumed three years later and completed on 18 November 1992.

Upgrading Mirage 2000s

The Mirage 2000EGs were fitted with Thomson-CSF RDM (Radar Doppler Multifunction) radar, which could not enable the aircraft to use Matra Super 530D medium-range, air-to-air missiles. Therefore, with the delivery of Matra Super 530Ds, the Mirage 2000BG/EGs had their radars upgraded to RDM-III, which could enable them to use these missiles. In addition to that, these Mirages were also equipped with an automated integrated Spirale chaff/flare countermeasures system (ICMS) at the same time.

In 1997, the Greek government ordered 50 AM.39 Exocet Block 2 anti-ship missiles, an air-launched variant of the MM.40 Exocet missile, which had been in service with the Hellenic Navy for coastal defence since 1993. To enable the Mirage 2000EGs to launch the missile, 18 of the RDM-3 radar-equipped Mirage 2000EGs were upgraded to Mirage 2000EG-SG3 (Standard Greece 3) by HAI in

Tanagra. They were serial numbers 210, 212, 213, 215, 216, 217, 218, 219, 220, 221, 222, 224, 226, 231, 232, 233, 237 and 242. These Mirage 2000EG-SG3s initially entered service with 331 Mira, which had also received the AM.39 Exocet Block 2 missiles earlier in 1998.

On 30 April 1999, the Greek government officially requested the purchase of 15 Mirage 2000-5 Mk.2s from France. Following approval, an order was placed, on 21 August 2000, for five Mirage 2000-5BGs and ten Mirage 2000-5EGs. In addition, ten of the old Mirage 2000EGs were to be upgraded by HAI to the Mirage 2000-5 Mk.2 standard.

Mirage 2000-5 Mk.2 is equipped with the more advanced RDY-2 radar, two main computers (MC1 and MC2) instead of the modular data-processing unit (MDPU) on the Mirage 2000BG/EG, a TOTEM 3000 laser gyro INS (Inertial Navigation System) instead of the mechanical ULISS system of the Mirage 2000BG/EG, three multi-function displays instead of an analogue instrument panel and an ICMS Mk.3 self-protection system instead of the old one.

New radar in the Mirage 2000-5 Mk.2 could enable use of the fire-and-forget MICA-RF active-radar homing medium-range air-to-air missiles instead of the old Matra Super 530D. In total, 100 MICA-RFs were ordered in 2000 with their deliveries taking place in 2003 and 2004. Later in 2003, 100 MICA-IRs, the heat-seeking short-range variant of the missile, were ordered with their deliveries taking place in 2006.

The RDM radars on HAF's Mirage 2000BG/EGs can detect a fighter jet-sized aerial target with five square meters RCS (Radar Cross Section) from 111km (60nm) distance and can engage enemy aircraft at look-down/shoot-down mode from 37km (20nm) distance to lock on one target and fire one or two Super 530F, and later Super 530D SARH, missiles.

The RDY radar can detect a fighter-sized target from 148km (80nm) distance and launch its missile from 80km (43nm) distance at four flying targets simultaneously. The RDY radar of the Mirage 2000-5BG/EG has significantly improved air-to-air and air-to-ground capabilities compared to the RDM, enabling pilots to use AM.39 anti-ship missiles instead to launch the MICA-RF (EM) through its maximum kill range. The radar could also be used for terrain following, enabling pilots to perform terrain-masking during low-level altitude in bad weather conditions as well as at night time for strike missions. In addition to these, the radar could also assist the use of SCALP EG cruise missiles by the aircraft. In total, 34 of these cruise missiles were purchased in 2004 with delivery taking place in 2007.

Ten Mirage 2000EGs with serial numbers 211, 214, 227, 230, 234, 235, 236, 240, 243 and 245 were modernized by the HAI to Mirage 2000-5EG Mk.2 standard between 2003 and 2007 and received serial numbers 511, 514, 527, 530, 534, 535, 536, 540, 543 and 545 after the upgrade, respectively. The upgraded Mirage 2000BG/EGs all received fixed inflight refuelling probes similar to the ones installed on the 15 new Mirage 2000-5 Mk.2s to enable them to receive fuel from the D-704 buddy refuelling pod equipped A-7E/TA-7Es.

The ten upgraded Mirage 2000-5EGs were delivered to 331 Mira between 2004 and 2007. Then on 1 March 2007, 331 and 332 MPK Squadrons were reorganized. The 331 Mira became the operator of the Mirage 2000-5BG/EG Mk.2s, and 332 Mira the operator of the Mirage 2000BGM/EGM-SG3s. A few months later, on 3 May 2007, the first Mirage 2000-5 Mk.2s were delivered. These new Mirage 2000-5BGs were serialled 505 to 509 while the Mirage 2000-5EGs received 546 to 555 serial numbers.

The ten ageing Mirage 2000EGs, which were upgraded by HAI, had a MilTech Hellas S.A. HDD-55L 5x5in head-down display with Active Matrix Liquid Crystal Display (AMLCD) technology installed as a replacement for their cathode ray tube (CRT) head-down displays. To install the HDD-55L, no further modifications were required to the Mirage 2000 or other associated aircraft systems.

Greek Mirage 2000s and Turkish F-16s

Two years after delivery of the Mirage 2000EGs, HAF began its deployment to Skyros Island to stand for quick reaction alert (QRA) duty. With the delivery of Mirage 2000-5EGs to 331 Mira, the majority of those deployments were performed by these RDY-2 equipped aircraft which were armed with two MICA-IR IRAAMs and two MICA-RF BVRAAMs each, while the old Mirage 2000EGs always had four R.550 Magic-2 IRAAMs after withdrawal of the Matra Super 530D missiles.

HAF's Mirage 2000s have engaged in hundreds of dogfights with THK's F-16C/Ds but only in one case have they shot down one of them. That took place on 8 October 1996, when a Mirage 2000EG with serial number 226 and piloted by Lt A Grivas engaged in a dogfight with an F-16D Block 40J of 192 Filo with serial number 91-0023, and shot it down using an R.550 Magic 2 missile in Greece airspace over the Aegean Sea.

The F-16D's student pilot, Captain Nail Erdogan was killed while the instructor pilot Lt Col. Osman Cıceklı ejected safely and was rescued 30 minutes after the crash by HAF's Agusta Bell AB.205A-1 SAR helicopter from the 358th Search and Rescue Squadron at Limnos. The pilot received immediate medical care and returned to Turkey a few days later. Information about this close encounter was kept secret from the public until 2003, when the Greek MoD revealed it and claimed it had happened due to a technical fault.

Several months after the failed Turkish military coup in July 2016, the Turkish Air Force significantly increased its flights into Athens FIR. Most of the time, the Mirage 2000-5EGs from 331 Mira assigned to the 135 Combat Group in Skyros intercepted the F-16C Block 40s of the 192 Filo 'Kaplan' based at 9th Main Jet Base of THK at Balikesir.

On 12 April 2018, a Mirage 2000-5EG, serialled 546, crashed almost nine miles northeast of Skyros Island after a dogfight with a Turkish F-16. The 546, together with a second Mirage 2000-5EG, had scrambled minutes before to intercept a pair of Turkish F-16Cs, which had violated Greek airspace. The aircraft collided with sea water and its pilot 1st Lt Giorgos Baltadoros lost his life. The reason for the accident is still unknown. It was the 13th and last Mirage 2000 lost to the HAF through its history.

On 3 May 2020, two F-16Cs harassed an Hellenic Army Aviation NH-90TTH helicopter over the Aegean Sea while it was carrying Greek Minister of Defence Nikolaos Panagiotopoulos and Chief of General Staff Konstantinos Floros during a visit to the Hellenic Army's surveillance outposts at Oinousses, Panagia, Agathonisi and Farmakonisi. Subsequently, two Mirage 2000-5EGs on combat air patrol (CAP) duty that day intercepted the F-16s. A video of their dogfight was released two days later and showed how the Mirage pilots had scored multiple missile locks on the F-16s during the dogfight.

In 2021, the Greek government ordered six Rafale DG/EG fighter jets from France. In the same year, the French government also agreed to supply Greece with 12 more Rafales free of charge as part of French military support for Greece. The Greek government ordered six more Rafale DG/EGs on 25 March 2022. Two Rafale DGs and four Rafale EGs were delivered to 332 Mira on 19 January 2022. They were part of the 12 Rafales that the French government agreed to deliver to Greece free of charge. The Greek government only paid the maintenance cost as well as the overhaul and modification work at the Dassault installation. Six months before delivery of the Rafale DG/EGs to 332 Mira, the squadron began reducing the number of its Mirage 2000BG/EGs from ten to six with their retirement taking place in December 2021.

Today HAF has five Mirage 2000-5BG combat trainers and 19 Mirage 2000-5EG multi-role fighter jets in 331 Mira's service, among them two thirds are operational simultaneously. Despite delivery of Rafale DG/EGs, HAF continues using Mirage 2000-5DG/EGs for QRA at both Tanagra and Skyros air bases. Another order for 18 to 24 Rafale DG/EGs in 2028 will allow HAF to retire its Mirage 2000-5s from service by 2030.

Delivered from June 1974, 40 Mirage F1CG fighter interceptors were operated by 334 and 342 Mira squadrons at Tanagra until their retirement in 2003. (Hellenic Air Force)

Two Mirage 2000EG-SG3s of HAF's 332 Mira squadron during a formation flight on 17 October 2008. This image shows 237 in front and 215 in the back. (Hellenic Air Force)

Serial number 212, operated by 332 Mira, was one of the last Mirage 2000EGM-SG3s to retire. It is departing Andravida Air Base for a mission during exercise Iniochos 2019. (Babak Taghvaee)

Serial number 217, a Mirage 2000EGM-SG3 from 332 Mira Squadron at Tangara, Greece, during the final months of its service in 2021. (Babak Taghvaee)

Serial number 231, a Mirage 2000EGM-SG3, was operated by 332 Mira Squadron until its retirement in 2021. It is departing Andravida for a night mission during exercise Iniochos 2019. (Babak Taghvaee)

AM.39 Exocet is the sole anti-ship missile used by the Mirage 2000s. Here, it is loaded on a Mirage 2000BG with serial number 201, previously operated by the 332 Mira Squadron. (Hellenic Air Force)

Mirage 2000-5EG Mk.2, with serial number 553, flies over Athens during the Independence Day parade on 25 March 2008. (Hellenic Air Force)

Mirage 2000-5BG, with serial number 506, from 331 Mira, during exercise Iniochos 2019. (Babak Taghvaee)

Mirage 2000-5BG, with serial number 507, from 331 Mira, under organizational level maintenance in the hangar at the Tanagra air base. (Babak Taghvaee)

A Mirage 2000-5EG Mk.2 from 331 Mira, with serial number 547, during departure from Tanagra Air Base in June 2019. (Babak Taghvaee)

A Mirage 2000-5EG Mk.2 from 331 Mira, with serial number 547, in front of an hardened aircraft shelter at Tanagra Air Base. (Babak Taghvaee)

Defenders of Aegean airspace: Rafale DG/EG multi-role fighter jets

On 19 January 2022, the first two Rafale DG combat-trainer aircraft and four Rafale EG multi-role fighter jets landed at Tanagra Air Base and were officially delivered to 332 Fighter Squadron of 114 Combat Wing. Delivery of the six Rafale F3-Rs took place just one year after the contract was finalised. The contract also included 12 second-hand examples from France.

With the rise in tensions between Greece and Turkey in the eastern Mediterranean Sea in 2020, the government of Greece increased its military cooperation with France to a strategic level to deal with the provocative actions of Turkey.

As a result of the Greece-France partnership and cooperation, the Greek government received an offer from France to immediately supply the Hellenic Air Force with 12 ex-French Air Force's Rafale B/Cs with an option for the sale of six brand-new examples from Dassault Aviation. Once the offer was accepted, the Greek Prime Minister Kryakos Mitsokatis announced the decision of the government on 12 September 2020.

On 25 January 2021, French Defence Minister Florence Parly travelled to Greece and met the Greek government and military officials including Prime Minister Mitsokatis. The parties signed the contract for the procurement of the 18 Rafale F3-R fighter jets. Earlier in 2020, the 4th and 30th Fighter Wings of the French Air and Space Force were each tasked to prepare one Rafale B and two Rafale Cs, mostly with F3 standard, for delivery to Dassault Aviation that year.

In order to prevent any shortage in operational aircraft within the fighter squadrons at Saint-Dizier and Mont-de-Marsan air bases in France, the decision was made to prepare one Rafale every two months for delivery to Dassault. The maintenance squadrons each carried out the full maintenance of each aircraft chosen for delivery to Dassault Aviation.

Preparing the Rafales for delivery

The aircraft chosen for delivery to Greece were the oldest examples with the highest number of flying hours recorded through their careers in the French Air Force. The first two aircraft were Rafale Bs with serial numbers 305 and 306. Both had been used for test and experimental purposes for years.

The 305 was in the service of the EC (Fighter Squadron) 1/4 'Gascogne' of 4th Combat Wing, while the 306 was in use with the ECE (Fighter Experiment Squadron) 1/30 'Côte d'Argent' under the control of the 30th Combat Wing. The 305 was a veteran of anti-ISIL Opération Chammal with seven precision guided bombs dropped during its final deployment to H4 Air Base in Jordan in 2019.

The first Rafale B, with serial number 305, was prepared for delivery by the maintenance squadron of the 4th Fighter Wing. The aircraft was capable of using ASMP-A nuclear cruise missiles and as a result 3,500 hours of maintenance work was required to remove 60 items of equipment specific to the French Strategic Air Forces before delivering the aircraft to the Dassault test facility in Istres, in January 2021.

Once converted to F3-R, the first Rafale, now designated as Rafale DG, received the Greek flag, HAF roundels and serial number 401 at Bordeaux, in May, and was delivered to the Hellenic Air Force during an official ceremony at Istres on 21 July 2022.

The sixth Rafale F3-R to serve the Hellenic Air Force was a Rafale EG, with serial number 413. It was upgraded to F3-R standard in December 2021 and was handed over to the HAF in the first week of January 2022. The two Rafale DGs with serial numbers 401 and 402, as well as the first four Rafale EGs with 410 to 413 serial numbers were flown to Greece on 19 January 2022.

The future of the Hellenic Rafale DG/EGs

The Hellenic Air Force received its first brand new Rafale EGs in July 2022 with serial numbers 450, 451 and 452. In December 2022, a fourth Rafale EG with serial number 453 was delivered to 332 Mira. As of January 2023, HAF was about to receive a brand new Rafale DG with serial number 441, while one more Rafale DG and another Rafale EG were near the end of their construction at the Dassault Aviation facility in Bordeaux.

Procurement and delivery of these Rafale F3-Rs enabled the HAF to establish air supremacy over the Aegean. The Rafale EGs, armed with MICA-NG and Meteor missiles, were due to be deployed to Skyros to support the Mirage 2000-5EG Mk.2s on QRA duty in spring 2023.

By the end of 2024, all deliveries will be complete. However, Mirage 2000-5BG/EG Mk.2s serving with the 331 Mira will also be replaced with 18 to 24 more Rafales starting in 2030.

The official handover ceremony of the first Rafale F3-R of the Hellenic Air Force was held at Istres Air Base, France, on 21 July 2021. The aircraft, serialled 401, a former Rafale B belonging to the French Air and Space Force, was delivered as a Rafale DG. (Greek Ministry of Defence)

Aircraft serial number 412, is a Rafale EG equipped with a captive training MICA-IR missile and a 2,000 litre external tank, shown here after a training mission, Bordeaux, France. (Babak Taghvaee)

From left to right are 412, 410 and 411, three Rafale EGs during the welcoming ceremony. (Babak Taghvaee)

Rafale DG with serial number 401 departing Bordeaux while armed with a captive training MICA-IR and loaded with two 1,250 litre external tanks for a 2v2 air-combat training on 14 December 2021. (Babak Taghvaee)

Rafale DG, with serial number 401, and customary water salute during the welcoming ceremony at Tanagra Air Base on 19 January 2022. (Babak Taghvaee)

Rafale DG, with serial number 402, and Dassault's instructor pilot in aft seat during the ferry flight from Istres, France, to Tanagra, Greece, on 19 January 2022. (Babak Taghvaee)

Rafale EG with serial number 410, is equipped with a captive training MICA-IR missile and a 2,000-litre external tank after a training mission from Bordeaux, France, on 15 December 2021. (Babak Taghvaee)

Rafale EG, with serial number 411, on the ramp of 332 Mira, on 19 January 2022. (Babak Taghvaee)

Rafale DG, with serial number 402, on the ramp of 332 Mira, on 19 January 2022. (Babak Taghvaee)

The first Rafale to touch down in Greece was handed over to the 332 Mira at Tanagra on 19 January 2022. It was Rafale EG with serial number 412. (Stam Pittas)

Chapter 2
The Water Bombers

Dromaders of Dekelia: PZL M-18B/BS fire-fighter aircraft
Since 1983, the 359 Public Services Air Support Unit (MAEDY) of HAF has been operated by PZL-Mielec M-18B Dromader aircraft for crop-dusting and fire-fighting purposes. Between March 1983 and January 1984, the squadron received 30 M-18Bs. To improve the quality of the pilot training, three two-seater M-18BS aircraft were also purchased, and delivered to the squadron in July 2002.

Since their delivery, the M-18Bs have assisted the larger fire-fighter aircraft, the CL-215s and later CL-415s in battling wildfires in summer. Due to the high intensity of their operations, the squadron has lost 12 aircraft in incidents and accidents between 1984 and 2021.

The M-18B can carry a maximum 2,500 litres (550 gallons) of water thanks to its powerful PZL Kalisz ASz-621R 9-cylinder air-cooled radial piston engine with 731 kW (980 hp) maximum power. The HAF has plans to procure 36 US-made Air Tractor AT-802 Fire Boss amphibious aircraft as a replacement for them under a programme with a 145 million euros budget until 2027.

Dromader pilot training
The Dromader pilots who fly at the 359 MAEDY are being trained at the 351 Aviation Applications Squadron (351 MAH) based in Tatoi airfield, Dekelia. The squadron is part of the 120th Air Training Wing of the HAF. In the past, when 359 MAEDY also operated Bell 47 helicopters and G.164A/G Ag-Cats, the 351 MAH had three companies each responsible for training pilots on the three types of aircraft. Nowadays, the squadron only trains the Dromader pilots. In addition, it is responsible for maintaining the flying skills of the pilots currently serving during the none-fire season, which is November to May.

Dromader pilots are categorised into three groups. First are the permanent reserve officers who are recalled and returned to active duty on the request of the General Staff; the second group are permanent officers of the air force who mostly serve in the 351 MAH as instructor pilots; and the third group are experienced civilian pilots, qualified for crop-dusting and fire-fighting operations. Leadership of the squadrons (commander and operations officer) are always chosen from the ranks of active permanent officers.

In July 2002, three M-18BS training aircraft were purchased specifically for M-18B pilot training at 351 MAH. The M-18BS are equipped with a water tank, which is smaller than that of the M-18B, but useful for trainees to practise water drops. After passing ground-school, each student passes several hours of training on the M-18BS. They first practise dropping small amounts of water and as they gain experience, the amount of water carried and dropped by their aircraft gradually increases. After completing 40 hours of training on the M-18BS, students continue flying solo with the M-18B until they gain enough skill to join 359 MAEDY.

Dromader operations during the fire season
During the fire-season, from 1 June to 31 October, 359 MAEDY has two to three M-18Bs on deployment at five to nine different airfields across Greece including Amygdaleona Kavala, Mytilene, Corfu, Kefalonia, Lamia, Tripoli, Sparta, Epitalia Ilia and Agrinio. These aircraft are maintained and operated by five or six different echelons, which carry out their missions completely independent of each other. Each echelon has its own mechanics who repair the aircraft at the deployment site without any need to redeploy them back to the home base at Tatoi.

The Dromader echelons carry out flights from 30 minutes before sunrise until 30 minutes after. They are not authorized to fly at night. Their ready to take-off time is 15 minutes. In fact, a Dromader pilot must be ready for flight in ten minutes after the task is assigned with most of this time allocated to performing the start-up checklist.

Dromaders are deployed for patrol flights during the 'dangerous' hours of the day when they carry 1.5 tons of water. Another Dromader with a larger amount of water in its water tank and a smaller amount of fuel in its fuel tanks is on high alert (15 minutes) at the airport. An M-18B usually carries 1,500kg of water but sometimes it increases to 2,200kg for the aircraft carrying less fuel.

As they are trained, the Dromader pilots usually drop water on fire from an average altitude of 10m (32ft), making it a dangerous task when they are flying with full tanks of water in mountainous regions. On 8 August 2021, a Dromader M-18B with serial number 128, hit a mountain while banking during a fire-fighting mission near Machairado, Zakynthos.

With the procurement of the Air Tractor AT-802F Fire Boss amphibian fire-fighter aircraft, the mission capabilities of 359 MAEDY will significantly improve. Equipped with a powerful P&W PT6A-67F turboprop engine producing 1,700 RPM with a Hartzell HC-B5MP-3F/M11276NS propeller, the AT-802F has a maximum 7.257kg (16,000lb) take-off weight. Thanks to that engine, it can carry a maximum 3,028 litres (800 gallons) of water or fire retardant, or a combination of both. In addition, it has a maximum fuel capacity of 1,438 litres (380 gallons). Its capacity to refill its water storage in the sea or nearby rivers will make the aircraft more functional when compared to the M-18B.

By the end of 2025, at least 30 AT-802Fs will be in the service of 359 MAEDY, and will carry out missions not currently tasked by the M-18Bs. As of January 2023, no official contract for AT-802F procurement had been reached. It is anticipated that following delivery of the new aircraft, the 359 MAEDY will to continue to operate M-18Bs into 2028 or 2029.

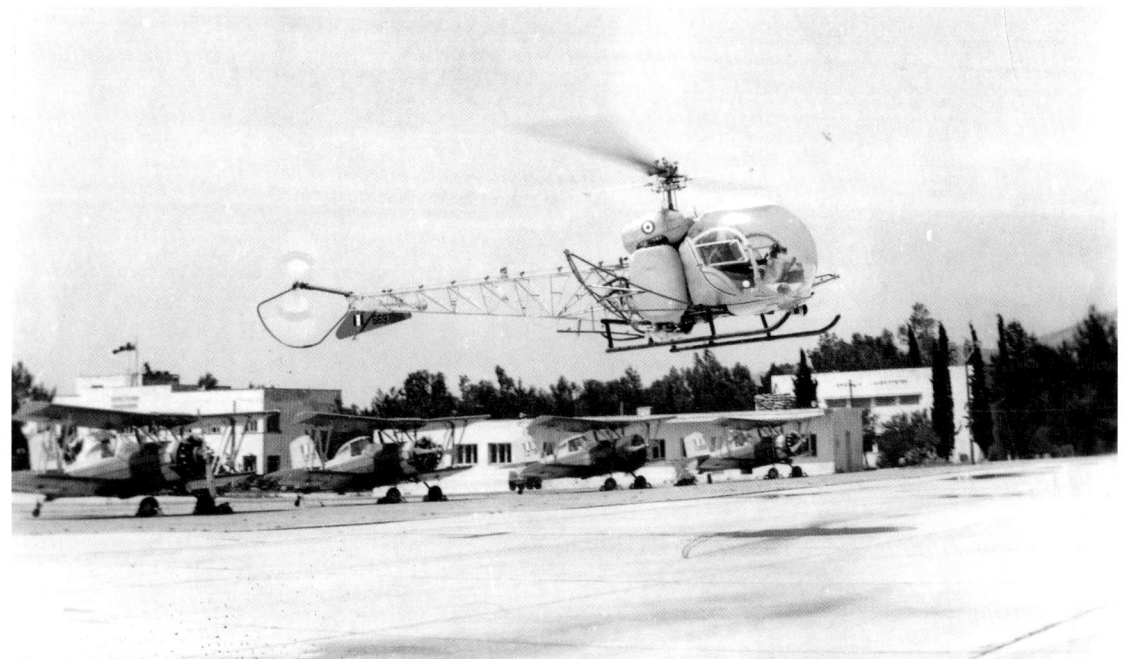

359 MAEDY, the current operator of PZL M-18B Dromader fire-fighter aircraft, once operated Bell 47 helicopters, including this Bell 47G-3B2A, with serial number 6697. This helicopter is flying in front of several Grumman G.164A/G Ag-Cats in Dekelia/Tatoi airfield in 1978. (Hellenic Air Force)

Serial number 1221 aircraft was one of the Grumman G.164A Ag-Cat crop-duster aircraft, which was operated by 359 MAEDY as a fire-fighter aircraft in the past. (Hellenic Air Force)

This PZL M-18B Dromader, with serial number 118 (c/n 1Z 011-18), is in service with 359 MAEDY during a fire-fighting exercise in May 2022. (Stam Pittas)

The Water Bombers

An M-18B Dromader of 359 MAEDY drops water during an exercise. (Hellenic Air Force)

One of three M-18BS training aircraft, serial number 806, in use for Dromader pilot training with 351 MAE. (Hellenic Air Force)

Water bombers of Elefsis: Canadair CL-215 fire-fighter aircraft

Out of the 39 fire-fighter aircraft operated by the Hellenic Air Force, eleven are Canadair CL-215s and are in service with 355 Tactical Transport Squadron (MTM) 'Vulcan' (Ifaistos) of 112 Combat Wing (PM) at Elefsis Air Base. They are the surviving examples of 20 CL-215s that HAF has received.

Between 1974 and 1979, the HAF received 11 CL-215GRs, which entered service with 355 MTM at Elefsis Air Base. Between 1983 and 1996, seven more CL-215s were purchased and received, and in 1995, four ex-Yugoslav Air Force examples were purchased and delivered two years later. These old but highly capable fire-fighter aircraft undertake a quarter of fire-fighting operations in Greece during every fire season.

In 1973, the Greek government placed an order for five CL-215 fire-fighter aircraft. Several months later, the first aircraft with registration code CF-TXH and construction number 1015, was delivered on 16 December 1973. Upon completion of training for the first Greek CL-215 pilots, this aircraft, and several more CL-215s were flown to Greece several months later.

The second aircraft, with construction number 1039, was delivered on 23 June 1974. Both were allocated to 355 TM (Transport Squadron) in December 1975. These CL-215s gradually replaced five ageing C-47A/B Dakotas, which were then converted into crop-duster aircraft. On 22 December 1975, the 355 TM was converted to MTM (Tactical Transport Squadron) following delivery of the CL-215s.

The original order was later increased to 11 aircraft. The nine remaining CL-215s, with construction numbers 1041, 1042, 1043, 1045, 1048, 1050, 1055, 1060 and 1064, were delivered between April 1976 and May 1979. In the Hellenic Air Force, their construction numbers became their serial numbers.

355 MTM continued operating C-47 Dakotas from Elefsis Air Base until 1984, when they were transferred to Sedes airport and operated by an independent squadron there. In addition to the Dakotas, the squadron received the last operational N2051D Noratlas transport aircraft from 354 MTM. In December 1983, the squadron received the Dornier Do-28 Skyservant, which allowed the ageing N2051Ds to retire. One remained operational, however, to be used as a navigation aid calibration aircraft until its retirement on 28 March 1987.

Challenging CL-215s operations

When fire-fighter aircraft approach the incident area, they are in contact with the commander of the aerial fire-fighting operation. The commander determines the tactics of attack and the escalation of the means, in cooperation with ground forces. Operations with the participation of aircraft from different agencies (HAF, Hellenic Fire Department and foreign aircraft and helicopters, observation aircraft and helicopters, and even the civilian aircraft flying nearby) create a very fluid environment. Conditions may be worsened by the reduced visibility caused by smoke. Therefore, clear and accurate information about the area on fire is paramount.

The Formation Leader, in addition to flying an aircraft, is responsible for obtaining a clear understanding of the tactical situation and the position of air assets and personnel on the ground. Ensuring fire-fighters are removed from the water drop area is important since dropping a heavy water load on to people from a short altitude can cause serious injury.

Large amounts of heat released by forest fire disrupt the local climate, creating unusual phenomena including strong turbulence, sudden updrafts and downdrafts and an increase in wind intensity, especially in mountainous areas. In some cases, a local increase in wind intensity by three units on the Beaufort scale above the prevailing wind in the wider area has been noted.

Due to the sudden and unexpected change of windspeed and temperature in the wildfire area, the crews check the drop area for obstacles and escape routes after the drop, taking into account the potential for engine stalling. Recognising the potential for turbulence, tornadoes and downdrafts is key.

Ensuring a safe water drop involves removing obstacles from the throw path of the aircraft, and after the water is released, the aircraft must be able to climb away avoiding obstacles such as tree tops. Dropping water in an uphill field and violating the minimum release altitude, or 32m (100 feet), for CL-215/415 aircraft, is prohibited.

Because of limited visibility, each aircraft's passage through the smoke must be carefully considered, especially in areas where it is unclear if anything is hidden by the smoke. Smoke also holds dangerous and strong turbulence, tornadoes and currents and, in the case of CL-415s, may cause problems with the operation of turboprop engines.

Nine of the 20 CL-215s delivered between 1973 and 1997 have been lost in incidents and accidents. In most cases, the cause was technical failure mainly in the aircraft's engine. By increasing the quality of maintenance, 355 MTM has reduced the number of incidents and accidents in recent years. Also, by increasing the quality of pilot training, crew errors have reduced.

As of January 2023, 355 MTM Squadron had 11 CL-215s in service (1039, 1041, 1043, 1045, 1055, 1060, 1067, 1069, 1073, 1110 and 1123). Seven of the ten CL-415s delivered in 1999 are also still in use with 383 MEEA in Thessaloniki. Six are CL-415GRs and one is a CL-415MP (Maritime Patrol). During each fire season, the CL-215s are dedicated to battling wildfires in Greece, while the CL-415s are often deployed to other European countries, as well as Israel, to assist other nations in battling wildfires.

1043 is one of 11 CL-215s from 355 MTM and is seen airdropping water during an exercise in May 2022. (Stam Pittas)

1069 is an ex-Yugoslav Air Force CL-215 still in service with 355 MTM and seen at its home base, Elefsis, in May 2022. (Hellenic Air Force)

1041, one of 355 MTM Squadron's CL-215s is under inspection at the maintenance hangar in April 2019. (Babak Taghvaee)

1110 is another ex-Yugoslav Air Force CL-215 seen during inspect or repair as necessary (IRAN) maintenance at Elefsis Air Base, in April 2019. (Babak Taghvaee)

Two of the last Dornier Do28D-2 Skyservant utility aircrafts used by 355 MTM are stored at Elefsis Air Base. (Babak Taghvaee)

Thessaloniki's water bombers: Canadair CL-415 multi-role aircraft

Since 30 January 1999, HAF has operated two types of Canadair CL-415 aircraft the fire-fighter version and the multi-role version. They were initially delivered to 355 Tactical Transport Squadron (MTM) in Thessaloniki, but since summer 2000, have been in service with 383 Special Operations and Air Fire-Fighting Squadron (MEEA) also in Thessaloniki. They have played an important role in battling wildfire in Greece and in many other EU member states as well as in Israel.

Between 1973 and 1990, HAF received 16 CL-215 fire-fighter aircraft, which entered service with 355 MTM at Elefsis Air Base. Five were lost in accidents and incidents. As a replacement, the Ministry of Agriculture procured four former Yugoslav Air Force's CL-215s from Slovenia, which were delivered in 1997. With the rising numbers of wildfires in Greece, the country needed more defensive aircraft and placed an order for ten CL-415s.

The order comprised eight CL-415GR fire-fighter aircraft and two CL-415MP multi-purpose aircraft with search and rescue capability. They were delivered between 30 January 1999 and 3 November 2004. 355 MTM became their operator. They were operated alongside the CL-215s until decisions were made to establish 383 MEEA in Thessaloniki to operate the CL-415s leaving the CL-215s with 355 MTM.

Superior capabilities of the CL-415s compared to the CL-215s

Equipped with two Pratt & Whitney Canada PW123AF turboprop engines, which produce 1,775kW (2,380hp) power, the CL-415 has better operational capabilities than the older CL-215, which has two Pratt & Whitney R-2800-83AM 18-cyl air-cooled radial piston engines producing 1,566kW (2,100hp) each.

Thanks to better engines, the CL-415 has a cruise speed of 333km/h (207mph, 180 kn), which is higher than the 291km/h (181mph, 15 kn) cruise speed of the CL-215. With the more powerful engines the aircraft can carry more water, fire retardant or a mixture of both. The CL-215 can carry a maximum 5,450 litres (1,561.3 gallons) while the CL-415 can carry 6,137 litres (1,621 gallons).

In addition, the aircraft has a modern, new generation cockpit, which uses liquid crystal displays (LCD) instead of analogue instrument gauges. It also has modern navigation and communication systems, a hydraulic-assisted control system, new electronically controlled water-release systems with four doors (instead of two,) which can release all of the water at once or sequentially, and more importantly, it has a mixing system for fire-retardant agents.

The CL-415MP variant can also be used for search and rescue missions. It is equipped with side-looking airborne radar (SLAR), and weather radar and forward-looking infrared (FLIR), which enable their use in search and rescue operations in all weather conditions, day and night. These aircraft also have a navigator, a flight mechanic and rescue personnel in addition to the pilot and co-pilot.

Thanks to the CL-415MP, the 383 MEEA has a close collaboration with the 31 Search and Rescue Operations Squadron and the Hellenic Navy Underwater Demolition Teams. Of the two CL-415MPs with serial numbers 2055 and 2056, today only 2056 exists in service after the other was lost in an accident in 2007.

Current fate of the CL-415 fleet

On 23 July 2007, 2055 was lost in an accident during a fire-fighting mission near Dilesos killing its pilot, Captain Dimitrios Stolidis and co-pilot 1st lt Ioannis Hadzoudis, a former Mirage 2000 fighter pilot. On that day, the aircraft was battling a fire in an olive grove near the village of Tsakeoi on Eboia island. Five aircraft and two helicopters were involved in the mission. The aircraft crashed into a mountain after failing to gain altitude after dropping water.

Out of the eight CL-415GRs and two CL-415MPs delivered to 383 MEEA, two CL-415GRs and one CL-415MP have been lost in one accident and two incidents. The CL-415MP lost in 2007 was 2055. The two CL-415GRs lost were 2039 and 2050. They were lost in non-fatal incidents on 26 April 2006 and 5 May 2014, respectively. The first aircraft was lost while being towed towards shore after an emergency landing in water. It flipped and sank off Chalkis, while the second flipped upon landing on water during a training mission near Aggelochori, Nea Michaniona, Thessaloniki.

Currently 383 MEEA Squadron has six CL-415GRs with serial numbers 2042, 2044, 2049, 2052, 2053 and 2054, and a CL-415MP with serial number 2056. All are operational simultaneously during the fire seasons. Out of season, most of the aircraft pass their A and B Level checks in the maintenance squadron at 113 Combat Wing though one or two CL-415s are kept operational for pilot-training purposes.

With the delivery of the CL-415s, the HAF began participating in international missions for battling wildfires. Such operations began on 18 August 1999, one day after the Izmit earthquake in Turkey, with a catastrophic magnitude of 7.6, which struck the Kocaeli Province, causing monumental damage and almost 20,000 deaths. The earthquake caused a fire in the Tupras petroleum refinery near Istanbul. 2042, a CL-415GR in service with 355 MTM, was deployed to Ataturk International Airport, Istanbul, and logged 15.5 hours of aerial fire-fighting in eight sorties dropping 320 tons of foam on burning refinery tanks.

2044 and 2054 are two of the seven surviving CL-415GRs and are seen during a formation flight. (Hellenic Air Force)

2044, a CL-415GR from 383 MEEA is air-dropping water during an exercise in May 2018. (Hellenic Air Force)

2049 was one of two CL-415GRs deployed to Cyprus to combat massive wildfires in the Troodos Mountains between 19 and 23 June 2016. (Babak Taghvaee)

A CL-415GR combating a wildfire in Troodos, Cyprus, in June 2016. (Babak Taghvaee)

2044 was one of two CL-415GRs deployed to Bordeaux, France, to battle a wildfire in August 2022. (Babak Taghvaee)

2044 can be seen scooping water during a fire-fighting mission in 2018. (Hellenic Air Force)

Hellenic Aerospace Industries is responsible for overhaul and depot maintenance of CL-415GR. 2054 is under overhaul in June 2019. (Babak Taghvaee)

Chapter 3

The Transport and Airborne Early Warning and Control Aircraft

Tactical airlifters of Elefsis: C-130B/H Hercules transport aircraft

The Hellenic Air Force operates four C-130Bs and ten C-130H Hercules Medium Transport Aircraft and all are in service with 356 MTM (Tactical Transport Squadron). Due to the Greek economic crisis, this small fleet of tactical transport aircraft faced serviceability issues resulting in a declining number of operational aircraft in service. With recent improvements in the economic situation and increased defence budgets, Hellenic Aerospace Industries (HAI) has started restoring and overhauling several C-130B/Hs, which were kept in storage.

Established on 19 December 1953, HAF's 356 Tactical Transport Squadron received 15 C-47A Dakota transport aircraft. With headquarters at Elefsis Air Base, west of Athens, the squadron is part of the 113th Combat Wing at Thessaloniki. In 1972, the squadron temporarily ceased its operations and its remaining airworthy aircraft were absorbed by other squadrons including 354 MTM, which had been established as a part of the 112th Combat Wing to operate Nord N2501D Noratlas.

On 29 September 1975, the first Lockheed C-130H Hercules landed at Elefsis piloted by the Greek crew, which had trained in the US. A few days later, 356 MTM was reformed. In addition to the 12 C-130s, the Squadron operated six ex-Olympic Airways Nihon Aircraft Manufacturing Corporation (NAMC) YS-11As, which were turboprop passenger/transport aircraft.

HAF's C-130Hs received serial numbers 741 to 752. For the first time in HAF's history, four of them, with serial numbers 744, 745, 746 and 747, participated in the Greek Independence Day parade while flying in formation on 25 March 1977.

One of HAF's C-130Hs with serial number 748 (c/n 4724) crashed on 5 February 1991 resulting in the death of all five crew and 58 passengers on board. The aircraft hit the side of Mount Othrys and was found three days later, around 24km (15 miles) southwest of Néa Anchialos Airport. At the time of the crash, the crew had lost orientation due to poor visibility caused by bad weather conditions.

Six years later, on 20 December 1997, another C-130H was lost; this time 750 (c/n 4729), which had been delivered in 1977. The aircraft had been assigned to a search and rescue mission to find the wreckage of a Yak-42 passenger aircraft belonging to Aerosvit Ukrainian Airlines with registration code UR-42334, which had gone missing on the approach to Thessaloniki three days earlier. While searching for the missing Yak-42, the C-130H hit a mountain while descending towards Tanagra Air Base.

To reinforce its small fleet of C-130Hs, in 1990 HAF opened negotiations with the United States to order the C-130Bs, which were being withdrawn from service from the USAF. Five C-130Bs with serial numbers 58-0723, 60-0296, 60-0300, 60-0303 and 61-0948, which had been operated by the USAF's 337th and 731st Tactical Airlift Squadrons (TAS) were delivered to 356 MTM. Ex-C-130Bs of 337th TAS were 60-0296 and 61-0948 while the other three belonged to the 731st TAS.

Upgrading the Hercules fleet by HAI

In 2004, SPAR Aerospace Ltd (L-3 SPAR) a subsidiary of L-3 Communications, began the modernisation of the first C-130H of the Hellenic Air Force at its facility in Edmonton, Canada, followed by the second C-130H at the HAI facilities in Tanagra. The second C-130H, which was upgraded to 'Hercules-2020 standard', was delivered to HAF during an official ceremony in the presence of the Chief of HAF's General Staff at HAI facilities on 21 December 2005.

The first C-130B upgraded to Hercules-2020 standard was delivered to HAF in summer 2006. Eight more C-130Hs and four more C-130Bs were scheduled to be upgraded to Hercules-2020 standard, however, due to Greece's financial crisis one C-130B was phased out of service, and modernisation of the remaining eight C-130Hs and three C-130Bs was delayed.

The Hercules 2020 programme had served to extend the life of the C-130s for 15 to 20 years at an affordable and competitive price but despite that, the restrained HAF budget caused delays to all C-130H upgrades to the Hercules-2020 standard. The upgraded C-130B/H (AUP) aircraft received the following:

- ARC-210 U/VHF radio
- New weather radar
- New autopilot system
- New navigational aid systems such as ILS, VOR/DMH, MB/TACAN
- Four large CRT displays instead of ADI (Attitude Data Indicator), HSI (Horizontal situation indicator) and weather radar for pilot and co-pilot
- Traffic collision avoidance system and its digital indicator for both pilot and co-pilot
- GPS receivers and a moving map (digital)

The above systems are interconnected with a MIL STD 1553 computer interface. In addition, the instrument panel and cockpit lighting were made compatible with the use of night-vision goggles (NVG) for night operations.

The current fate of the Hercules fleet

The C-130Hs and C-130Bs have been tasked with several humanitarian relief operations in addition to their traditional task of performing joint search and rescue operations with the 31st Search and Rescue Operations Squadron (SAROPS). These missions have been for post-disaster relief as well as fire-fighting. For example, after the Kalamata earthquake on 13 September 1986, the Kozani earthquake on 13 May 1995 and the Parnitha earthquake on 7 September 1999, C-130s airlifted medical teams to affected regions.

Greece's C-130B/Hs have transferred humanitarian aid provided by Greece's Red Cross to regions across the world to people affected by disasters, including earthquakes and tsunamis. After the powerful 7.7 magnitude earthquake at Rudbar, northern Iran on 20 June 1990, which led to the deaths of 50,000 people and injuries to 60,000 others, the HAF dispatched a C-130H loaded with several tons of medical aid, to Tehran.

In March and April 1991, at the beginning of Gulf War I, 771,000 Kurds and Shiites crossed the border to Iran on 12 April 1991, while one million refugees went to Turkey. The HAF sent five C-130Hs to the west of Iran with several tons of food, medicine, clothing, tents and blankets. They were the first aircraft of the European Red Cross to bring aid to the Kurdish refugees.

One of the most recent humanitarian relief missions involving an HAF Hercules took place on 19 September 2022, when 747, a C-130H, carried several tons of medical supplies, tents, surgical gloves, blankets and sleeping bags to Karachi for people in the flood-affected regions of Pakistan. In addition to these humanitarian relief missions, C-130B/Hs have assisted the CL-215, CL-415 and M-18B Dromader fire-fighting aircraft with wildfires in Greece.

In December 1975, the HAF received its first five CL-215GRs, which entered service with 355 MTM Squadron at Elefsis Air Base. In 1996, four more examples were purchased from Yugoslavia, and three years later, the first CL-415s were delivered to the HAF. 356 MTM assisted its neighbouring 355 MTM in fire-fighting missions thanks to three Modular Airborne Fire-fighting System (MAFFS), which were used on the C-130s.

With the help of the MAFFS, a C-130B/H can carry 19,500lbs of fire retardant or water and release that in ten seconds by means of two tubes through two side Paratrooper doors on both sides of the aircraft. It takes three to four hours to load a MAFFS system on a C-130B/H and only 12 minutes to fill it with water or fire retardant or a mixture of both.

In January 2023, HAF had two operational C-130Hs, which were 747 and 752, and was awaiting delivery of two C-130Bs with serial numbers 723 and 948, which had recently been overhauled and upgraded by the HAI and SPAR Aerospace Ltd in Tanagra. Thanks to the increase in the defence budget of Greece, overhaul and restoration of three out of seven C-130B/Hs in storage at Tanagra has started. In addition to the plans for increasing the number of airworthy C-130B/Hs, HAF's General Staff was studying plans to buy six C-130J-30s from the United Kingdom.

This image shows a tactical formation flight of two C-130Hs of 356 MTM with serial numbers 743 and 749, on 20 June 2007. At that time, the C-130s were still in Vietnam War-era camouflage. (Hellenic Air Force)

745 is a C-130H currently awaiting overhaul at Tanagra Air Base. (Babak Taghvaee)

747 is one of the two airworthy C-130Hs of 356 MTM, which was delivered to the squadron following overhaul and restoration in 2021. (Babak Taghvaee)

752 is one of the C-130Hs from 356 MTM and can be seen at Larnaca International Airport, Cyprus, during an exercise in November 2021. (Babak Taghvaee)

Cypriot paratroopers can be seen jumping out of a C-130H with serial number 752, during an exercise in Cyprus in November 2021. (Babak Taghvaee)

751, C-130, of 356 MTM is seen flying over Elefsis Air Base in October 2018. (Babak Taghvaee)

948 is one of the four surviving C-130Bs. It is seen here in its old branding in Elefsis in 1998. (Hellenic Air Force)

404 is one of two Beechcraft 350C King Air Ambulance Aircraft used by the National Centre for Emergency Care (EKAB) since 2022. 356 MTM operates these two aircraft. (Modestos Meletiou)

Hellenic Spartans: C-27J Spartan transport aircraft

354 'Pegasus' Tactical Transport Squadron (MTM) based at Elefsis Air Base, has operated eight Alenia C-27J Spartan medium-sized STOL transport aircraft since 2015. Like 356 MTM, the 354 MTM has struggled with a low number of operational C-27Js due to the Greek financial crisis.

Today, only two out of the eight C-27Js are operational. However, following a contract finalised by the Greek General Directorate of Defence Equipment and Investments (GDAEE) with Leonardo SpA on 7 July 2022, the restoration, overhaul and upgrade of six C-27Js kept in storage for years has started. In four years' time, the Hellenic Air Force will have six operational C-27Js simultaneously.

The HAF was one of the largest operators of the C-47A/B Skytrain light transport aircraft in Europe. While all NATO air powers replaced their C-47s with more modern aircraft, the HAF continued operating existing aircraft until 2008 when the last operational example was withdrawn from service. Gradually they have been transferred from a tactical transport role through the 1990s and replaced with five ageing ex-USAF C-130Bs.

To relieve the C-130B/H fleet of missions previously carried out by the C-47s, Greece ordered 12 C-27J Spartan tactical transport aircraft from Italy in January 2003, with delivery commencing in 2004. Four aircraft were cancelled leaving eight to be delivered with serial numbers 4117, 4118, and 4120 to 4125.

To operate the C-27Js, 354 MTM 'Pegasus' was reorganized by the HAF at Elefsis Air Base, on 12 January 2005. The squadron had previously been suspended on 18 April 1982 with its last Nord N2501D Noratlas aircraft transferred to 355 MTM. The squadron was the largest operator of ex-Luftwaffe (West German Air Force) N2501Ds in the 1970s. In total, 51 had been delivered from West Germany as part compensation for the damages of World War Two. Twenty of these aircraft were deployed to Souda following the Turkish invasion of Cyprus during Operation *Atilla* in July 1974.

On 21 July 1974, 13 N2501Ds from 354 MTM participated in Operation Niki to recapture and liberate Nicosia airport, Cyprus. They carried airborne commandos from the 1st Rangers Squadron of the Hellenic Army. During operations, four N2501Ds were lost. One was shot down by friendly fire near the airport killing four crew members and 27 commandos on board. One crash-landed following double engine failure and led to the death of two commandos on board, while the other two aircraft, which could not be flown back to Greece after landing at Nicosia airport, were blown up by the pilot and co-pilot of another Noratlas.

354 MTM continued operating Noratlas until July 1980 when its remaining operational aircraft were delivered to 355 MTM. The squadron was disbanded on 18 April 1982 then re-formed 23 years later on 3 January 2005, in order to operate the 12 (later reduced to eight) new C-27Js. After the end of the test flight of the first C-27J, and on completion of training for the first group of pilots, the first aircraft arrived at Elefsis Air Base and a re-establishment ceremony was held for the squadron on the same day on 10 October 2005.

The first group of C-27 pilots (all with rank of lieutenant) were trained in Italy between November 2004 and March 2005. They passed ground school, flight simulator training and flight training with the first C-27J. The second group of four pilots had their ground school in Greece in May and June 2005 and then simulator training in Italy in July 2005, with flight training with the Italian Air Force between August and October 2005.

Equipped with two Rolls-Royce AE 2100D2 turboprop engines with Dowty R-391-F/10 six-bladed propellers each producing 4,637hp thrust, the aircraft could have a 32,500kg (71,650lb) maximum take-off weight. With 1,759km (1,093 miles) of operational radius and 5,852km (3,636 miles, 3,160 nmi) of ferry range thanks to its 77,000 litres (20,500 gallons) maximum fuel capacity, the aircraft can carry 6,000–11,300kg (13,200–24900lb) of payload to all Greek islands of the Aegean and Mediterranean, as well as Cyprus.

The current fate of the Spartan fleet

As of January 2023, the two operational C-27Js with serial numbers 4117 and 4121 were used for logistic support missions such as transporting military personnel and equipment between Greece's mainland and various islands. The same mission is performed by two operational C-130H Hercules aircraft with serial numbers 747 and 752. In addition to the logistic support, the aircraft are in use for VIP transport inside Greece and to other countries.

In December 2022, the HAF began studying plans for the procurement of six second-hand Hercules C4 (C-130J-30) medium-size tactical transport aircraft from the Royal Air Force which will be retired from service in 2023. Equipped with four Rolls-Royce AE 2100D3 turboprop engines and six-bladed Dowty R391 composite constant-speed fully feathering reversible-pitch propellers similar to the ones on C-27Js, the ex-RAF C-130J-30s can fill the gap in the HAF's service until delivery of new transport aircraft such as the A400M for which procurement negotiations are ongoing.

4117 is one of eight C-27Js from 354 MTM that can be seen at Alenia's aircraft factory prior to handover to the air force on 24 February 2005. (Hellenic Air Force)

4121 was one of only two active C-27Js in 2019; it can be seen in then main ramp of the squadron, in Elefsis, in April 2019. (Babak Taghvaee)

The front view of C-27J with serial number 4121 at Elefsis Air Base shows two Rolls-Royce AE 2100D2 turboprop engines with Dowty R-391-F/10 six-bladed propellers. (Babak Taghvaee)

4122 is currently one of the C-27Js from 354 MTM, which was airworthy until 2018. It is landing at Larnaca Airport in April 2018. (Babak Taghvaee)

4117 is currently one of two airworthy C-27Js from 354 MTM. It is departing Bordeaux for Elefsis in August 2022. It was used to transport groundcrews from 383 MEEA from Thessaloniki to maintain and operate two CL-415s that were deployed to France to combat wildfires in the Gironde region. (Babak Taghvaee)

4120 is a C-27J currently being overhauled at Elefsis Air Base. (Babak Taghvaee)

Erieyes of Elefsis: Embraer EMB-145H airborne early-warning and control aircraft

Established on 25 June 2001, 380 Airborne Early Warning & Control System Squadron (ASEPE Mira) operates four Embraer EMB-145H Airborne Early Warning and Control (AEW&C) Aircraft, which play an important role in protecting Greek air space. Equipped with the Erieye radar system developed by Saab Electronic Defence Systems of Sweden, the aircraft is capable of monitoring airspace within 450km (280 miles), which enables the air force to monitor the Turkish Air Force over the west of Turkish air space, and to provide a surveillance capability for NATO to monitor the activities of its adversaries over the Black, Aegean and Mediterranean seas.

In 1998, HAF's General Staff announced its plans for procuring an AEW&C platform. On 1 July, a contract was finalized between the General Directorate of Equipment and Ericsson-Thomson CSF AEW Systems. Under the contract, companies Erricson (Now SAAB), Thompson (Now Thales) and Embraer could receive euros 530 million to provide four AEW&C aircraft using the Embraer EMB-145 platform and Erieye radar system.

The Erieye radar system provides 300-degree coverage and instrumental range of 450km (280 miles) plus a detection range of 350km (210 miles) in a dense, hostile, electronic warfare environment in heavy radar clutter and at low target altitudes. The radar system has an integrated identification of friends or foe (IFF) system and capability, and can perform sea surveillance too. In addition, EMB-145Hs have a passive earth system model electronic support measures (ESM) system for detecting, locating, analysing and recording electromagnetic radiation in the 2-18 GHz spectrum.

Implementation of the contract took place in two phases. The first phase (interim solution) included the temporary lease of two SAAB-340H AEW&C aircraft belonging to the Swedish Air Force starting from 12 and 18 months after signing the contract, while the second phase involved the delivery of four EMB-145Hs equipped with the same radar systems previously installed on the SAAB-340Hs. The SAAB-340Hs were actually two Argus S100Ds of the Swedish Air Force with serial numbers 10003 and 10004, which were in use by the 72nd Squadron of the air force from 1996.

To operate the AEW&C aircraft, HAF created the 380 Airborne Early Warning & Control System Squadron (ASEPE Mira) 'Uranus' at Elefsis Air Base on 6 June 2001. The first SAAB-340H, with tail code 004, arrived at Elefsis on 30 June 2001 and was delivered to 380 ASEPE Mira five days after the squadron's establishment in 112 Combat Wing (PM). A few weeks later, the second aircraft, with tail code 003, was delivered earlier than planned. On 25 September 2001, the squadron put both aircraft into operation after completing their acceptance tests. They remained in service until delivery of the EMB-145Hs began.

The first EMB-145H, with 671 serial number, arrived at Elefsis on 29 October 2004. After delivery of the remaining four aircraft, they began flying with the first article acceptance test (FAAT 3) from 4 September 2006. On 5 May 2008, the Operational Test Evaluation (OTE) flights came into effect for the final evaluation of the EMB-145H platform. These were successfully completed on 23 June 2008. From 18 July of that year, HAF started operating its first EMB-145H with a fully operational and functional Erricson Erieye AEW system. Just a few days later, the aircraft participated in the first joint exercise 'Parmenion 2008'. Then from 15 to 19 December 2008, HAF performed an initial regular evaluation of the squadron.

According to a support contract signed in 2008, SAAB would maintain and supply spare parts for the Erieye AEW radar system and other electronic components installed on the EMB-145Hs for 20 years continuing until October 2028. The radar system has a one-year warranty, which is upgraded each year to guarantee follow-on-support (FOS) and ensure a high level of support and operational availability of the aircraft.

The current fate of the EMB-145H fleet

The Hellenic Air Force has two EMB-145Hs operational simultaneously while two others are under maintenance at Tanagra. Of the two operational aircraft, one is always ready for operations at any time and anywhere during the week while the other is a reserve aircraft; however, at times 380 ASEPE Mira has had both aircraft engaged in two different missions simultaneously.

On 6 June 2006, they displayed their capacity for interoperability and information sharing with other NATO air assets during operational tests when an EMB-145H successfully connected the French Navy aircraft carrier, *Charles de Gaulle* and a British and French Navy Frigate using Link 11 and 16 datalinks. It was the first time that an AEW&C aircraft had its Link-16 datalink terminal connected to other European military equipment. This occurred north of the Karavia Missile Test Range in Crete.

From 9 to 16 November 2006, an EMB-145H participated in a NATO-led electronic warfare exercise 'Trial Spartan Hummer'. A NATO E-3A AWACS, a French E-3CF AWACS, a USAF RC-135W, an Italian Tornado ECR Electronic Warfare aircraft and a Canadian Navy frigate were also involved in the exercise. During this exercise, for the first time, an EMB-145H acting as an airborne command-and-control asset used Link-16 datalink to transfer information to non-command-and-control platforms involved in the exercise.

Today, the flights performed by the EMB-145Hs of 380 ASEPE Mira are categorized in three parts. The first are training ones usually lasting from two to a maximum of four hours while the others are daily surveillance missions which last from four to a maximum of eight hours. These missions are performed for the benefit of the Hellenic Armed Forces in order to gather intelligence about the activities of Turkish Armed Forces around the Aegean and Mediterranean seas. Those missions performed in support of NATO's joint operation focuses on gathering intelligence that can be shared by military units of other forces operating in the region.

From 22 June 2015 to 31 March 2020, The European Union Naval Force Mediterranean (EU NAVFOR Med) carried out Operation 'Sophia' to neutralize established refugee smuggling routes in the Mediterranean Sea. 380 ASEPE Mira supported the naval forces from Belgium, France, Germany, Italy, Netherlands, Ireland, Slovenia, Spain and the United Kingdom during the operation. Its aircraft performed several weekly sorties and searched via Erieye radar-equipped EMB-145Hs for suspicious vessels carrying immigrants.

Today, the 380 ASEPE Mira continues to monitor the activities of the Turkish Air Force, Navy and Coast Guard in the Aegean and Mediterranean seas and the Turkish mainland as well as assisting NATO's naval forces in monitoring the activities of the Russian Navy and Air Force, and monitoring the Mediterranean Sea for immigrants and weapons. To keep this squadron's personnel at the highest state of readiness, the military take part in the annual joint Exercise Iniochos. During these exercises a range of missions is rehearsed including acting as an airborne control centre for airborne early-warning aircraft. At the same time, a second EMB-145H flies missions over the Aegean Sea ensuring there are no threats to the aircraft participating in these exercises.

A formation flight of four HAF fighter jets comprising an A-7E, a Mirage 2009-5BG Mk.2, an F-4E and an F-16D over Kranias gunnery range during exercise CAMPEROS 2014 on 7 March 2014. (Greek Ministry of Defence)

729 is one of four EMB-145Hs and is taxiing towards the runway at Elefsis AB for a mission in April 2019. (Babak Taghvaee)

734 is one of four EMB-145Hs and is shown in the hangar of 380 ASEPE Mira, in Elefsis, in April 2019. (Babak Taghvaee)

VIP carriers of Elefsis: ERJ-135LR, Gulfstream V and Falcon 7X business jets

The Hellenic Air Force has three business jets, which are operated by 352 VIP Transport Squadron (MMYP). These aircraft, comprising an Embraer EMB-135LR, a Gulfstream-V and a Dassault Falcon 7X, are in use to transport Greek government and military officials.

In 1999, a decision was made to form the 3rd VIP Wing within the HAF to operate the existing C-130B/Hs of 356 MTM and the VIP Helicopters of 358 MED for VIP flights of the Greek government and military, when needed. In 1999, HAF received an Embraer ERJ135LR with construction number (c/n) 145209, which later received serial number 145-209, in service of the force. ERJ-135LR was a long-range version of the ERJ135 regional jet with increased fuel capacity and upgraded engines (Rolls-Royce AE3007A1P turbofan each with 8,169lbf thrust). The Belgian Air Force was the launch customer of this aircraft.

The first VIP transport mission, with the Embraer EMB-135LR, took place on 9 March 2000 when the aircraft was used to transfer the Minister of National Defence to Brussels. Two years after that, HAF received a second VIP aircraft, an ERJ135BJ legacy aircraft, with c/n 145484. It received serial number 135L-484 and was superior to EMB135LR being equipped with two Rolls-Royce BR700-710A1-10 turbofans, each with 14,700lbf thrust.

The new ERJ135BJ was used for the first time to transport the Greek Minister of Finance to Copenhagen on 6 September 2002. In January 2003, a VIP Transport Squadron was formed incorporating the two ERJ135s, which were previously operated by the 356 MTM for the 3rd VIP Transport Wing. Later that year, a Gulfstream-V, with serial number 678, joined the squadron. Equipped with two Rolls-Royce BR700-710A1-10 turbofans, each with 14,700lbf thrust, the aircraft could carry a maximum of 12 people in comparison to the ERJ135s, which could each

Gulfstream V with serial number 678 was once the primary VIP aircraft used by Greek government officials. It is now the backup aircraft for the Falcon 7X of 352 VIP Transport Squadron. The Greek Prime Minister is on board during landing at Larnaca Airport on 24 January 2019. (Babak Taghvaee)

carry 15 people. The Gulfstream-V was used for the first time to transport the Greek Prime Minister to Brussels on 26 March 2003.

In May 2008, the VIP Transport Squadron (MMYP) was designated the number 352. In 2021, Dassault Aviation gifted a Falcon 7X VIP aircraft to the HAF, which entered 352 MMYP's service. Equipped with three Pratt & Whitney Canada PW-307A turbofan engines, each producing 6,402lbf of thrust, and seats for 12 passengers, the aircraft has a maximum service ceiling of 51,000ft and a maximum speed of Mach 0.90. The aircraft, which was painted Gunship Grey, had serial number 273.

With the delivery of the Falcon 7X, the Greek government donated the ERJ135BJ of 352 MMYP to the Government of Cyprus in September 2022. The aircraft was painted in new colours and received serial number CAF-001 on its vertical stabilizer. It was used for the first time by the Cypriot government officials who travelled to London to attend the funeral of HM Queen Elizabeth II.

EMB-135LR with serial number 145-209 is in front of Gulfstream V with serial number 678, from 352 VIP Transport Squadron at Elefsis Air Base in April 2019. (Babak Taghvaee)

Chapter 4
Training Aircraft

Basic pilot trainers of Dekelia: Tecnam P2002-JF training aircraft

In 2023, the Hellenic Air Force had 62 training aircraft in service comprising 13 Tecnam P2002 JF Sierra basic pilot trainers, 43 Beechcraft T-6A Texan II intermediary pilot trainers and 12 North American Rockwell T-2C/E Buckeye advanced jet trainers. The T-2s are to be withdrawn from service in 2023 giving their place to ten Alenia Aermacchi M-346B master advanced jet trainers. Under a contract finalized on 5 January 2021, these aircraft are used by a flight academy modelled on the Israeli Air Force's pilot-training centre by Elbit Systems Ltd to train future fighter pilots. The current fate of aircraft pilot training in the HAF and the role of training aircraft such as P2002-JF, T-6A and M-346B are reviewed here.

First year student pilots in the air force are trained on Tecnam P2002-JF training aircraft at 360 Flight Training Squadron (MTE). P2002-JF is a two-seat, single engine, low-wing, light aircraft equipped with a tricycle fixed landing gear, a Bombardier Rotax 912 S2 piston engine with maximum thrust of 98.5hp at 9,500rpm thanks to its variable pitch propeller. The squadron operates 12 of these aircraft, which were purchased in October 2018 with the first three delivered on 12 June 2019.

In 1947, HAF received 17 De Havilland DH82A Tiger Moth II basic trainers from the UK as military aid. Equipped with a Gipsy Major piston engine with 150hp power, they remained in service until 1955. T6776, which was one of them, is the sole surviving example today, and is preserved in the Hellenic Air Force Museum at Tatoi. (Hellenic Air Force)

With a maximum speed of 142 knots (263km/h), a service ceiling of 4,600m (14,000 feet), a maximum take-off weight of 620kg (1367lb) and maximum range of 568nm (1,051km), Tecnam P2002-JF succeeded the Cessna T-41D, which was retired from service on 20 December 2022.

Back in 1969, HAF received 21 T-41Ds under the US Military Aid Program as a replacement for its ageing North American T-6D/G Texan/Harvard training aircraft. Equipped with a Continental 0-360-D six-cylinder piston engine capable of producing 210hp power, the T-41Ds were one of the best basic pilot-training aircraft of their time. Collectively they logged 200,000 flight hours through their careers in the 360 MTE and only three of them were lost including on 1 February 1972 (69-7189), 17 September 2005 (69-7181) and 13 May 2013 (69-7196).

HAF also operated the T-41Ds for observation and surveillance missions in order to detect wildfires around Athens during fire season. These missions were performed by civilians and military instructor pilots serving in the squadron. HAF continued using them for this purpose until 2022. When the type was officially withdrawn from service in December 2022, the 360 MTE still had nine of the original 21 airworthy T-41Ds, which were 69-7182, 69-7187, 69-7190, 69-7192, 69-7193, 69-7194, 69-7195, 69-7199 and 70-1962.

Each student pilot must log 16 sorties on Tecnam P2002-JF before their solo flight. After that, they log another 19 flights. The total number of flying hours logged by each student pilot at the 360 MTE varies between 40 and 50 hours. After graduation from the basic flight training course at Dekelia, the students are sent to Kalamata Air Base to continue their training on the Beechcraft T-6A Texan II.

In the years between 1947 and 1969, HAF operated British Harvard Mk.II A/B and Mk.III training aircraft and their American and Canadian licence-built versions, which were T-6D/G Texan and AT-16ND respectively. In total, 108 of these were delivered of which 33 were AT-16ND. FX413 was one of them. (Hellenic Air Force)

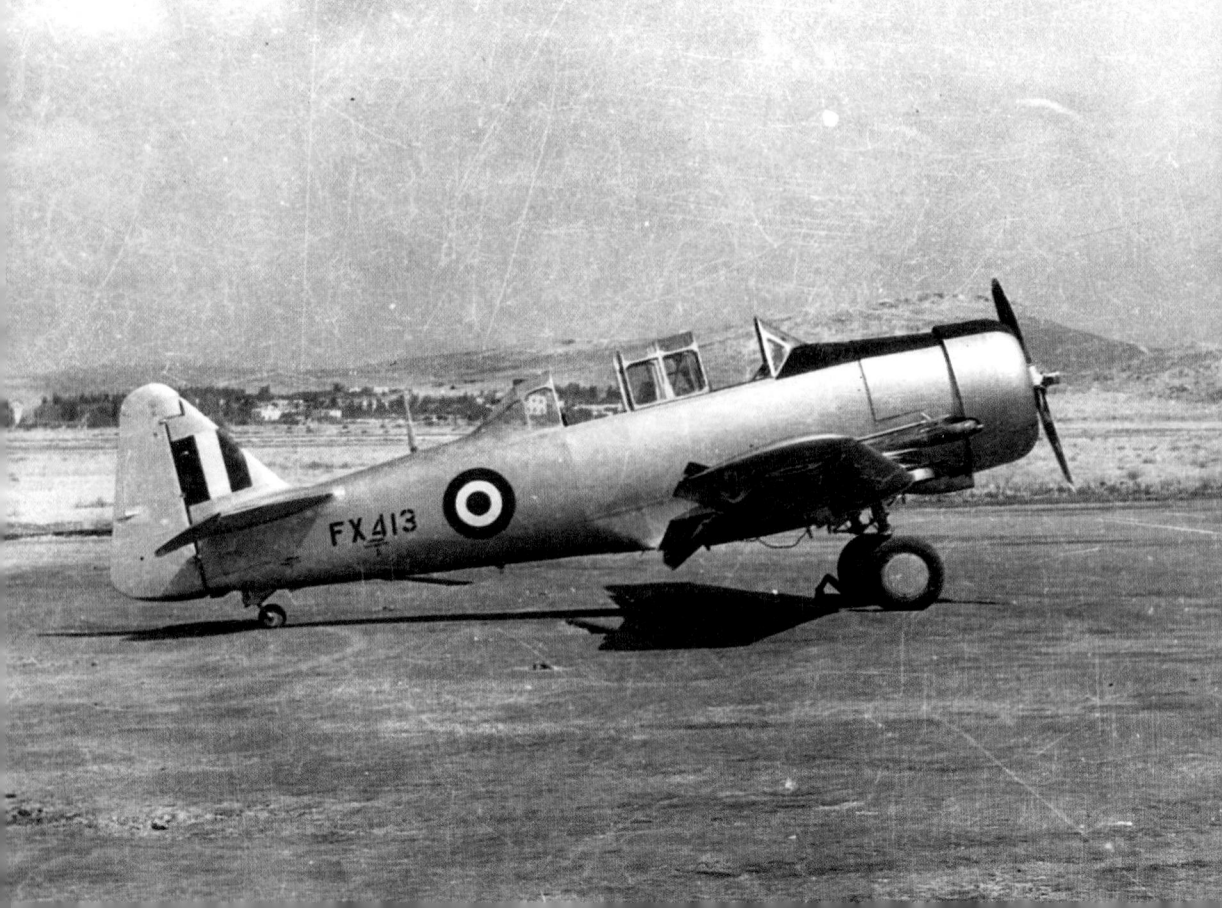

HAF operated 21 Cessna T-41Ds as basic training aircraft until December 2022. This aircraft, 69-7197, was one of them. (Hellenic Air Force)

On 12 June 2019, HAF received its first three Tecnam P2002-JFs during a ceremony at Dekelia/Tatoi airfield. (Greek Ministry of Defence)

The handover ceremony of the first three Tecnam P2002-JF basic training aircraft to the HAF was on 12 June 2019. (Greek Ministry of Defence)

Two of the first three Tecnam P2002s at the handover ceremony at Tatoi/ Dekelia on 12 June 2019. (Greek Ministry of Defence)

The Turbotrainers of Kalamata: T-6A/B Texan II training aircraft

HAF began searching for a replacement for its T-37B/Cs in the 1990s primarily to reduce costs and improve the quality of pilot training. Beechcraft T-6A/B Texan II, the same aircraft that was going to replace T-37Bs in the USAF, was selected to replace the T-37s. A contract to procure 45 was finalised in 1999 at a cost of US$223 to 240 million, with delivery of the first batch to 361 Basic Training Squadron scheduled for 31 July 2000. With their delivery, the squadron split, with one half continuing to operate the T-37s while the second company, which formed on 21 August 2000, operated the first batch of T-6A Texan IIs. The last group of T-37s retired in October 2002.

Initially, 14 instructor pilots, all former T-37 instructors, were trained on the T-6A. Their training completed on 16 September 2001. From 6 June to 17 July 2002, the squadron also used the T-6As to train the first group of air doctors. Immediately following retirement of the final T-37s, the squadron received 20 T-6Bs, which were armed variants of the T-6A, capable of carrying gun and rocket pods as well as bombs making them suitable for gunnery and weaponry training.

Thanks to the T-6Bs, the 361 Basic Training Squadron participated in protection operations for the Athens Olympics. All of its instructors were trained by the School of Tactical Weapons for air-to-air and air-to-ground missions against slow-moving targets. During the Olympic Games, the armed T-6Bs flew over Athens from dawn to dusk.

In 2005, a T-6A aircraft demonstration team was established in 361 Basic Training Squadron. The team named 'Daedalus' operated the T-6A/Bs once its pilots were trained by two instructors from the USAF, Captain Jeff Stift, instructor of the West Coast Demo Team, and Captain Eric McUmper, Ground-Flight Safety Observing Officer of the East Coast Demo Team.

The USAF instructors trained five T-6 instructor pilots and two were selected to perform the first display flight during the 1st International Air Show 'Archangel' on 18 September 2005. They were Major (I) Nikolaos Chrystopoulos and Major (P) Nikolaos Malapanis. In training they logged 18 flights with their instructors and 12 solo flights accumulating 20.8 flying hours.

In 2006, 361 Basic Fight Training Squadron had its name changed to 361 Flight Training Squadron (MEA). In that year, the air force's flight training programmes changed to accommodate two stages: primary and basic. Because of the high number of instructors and aircraft in 361 MEA, the squadron split and 364 MEA was created in March 2006.

Missions performed by the new squadron matched those of 361 MEA. However, as part of the implementation of the Hellenic-Italian Air Exchange Training Agreement in 2008, four Italian Flight Instructors are employed at 364 Air Training Squadron, and six to ten Italian student pilots are trained annually.

Today, 361 and 364 MEAs have 45 T-6A/B Texan IIs at their disposal of which 30 are always operational. Among the 15 other aircraft, six may be under organization and depot-level maintenance while the rest are in storage ready to be brought into service if needed.

Today, both 361 and 364 MEA squadrons train pilots in two phases. During the Initial Phase II, the training aims to improve pilot skills in manoeuvres as well as aircraft system management to ensure compliance with safety rules and decision making in all flight conditions. Basic Phase II training enhances prior knowledge and flight skills and develops leadership skills, team building and team spirit, as well as setting the foundations for aviation consciousness with information management and situational competence.

During the Initial Phase II training, students log 48 sorties over 60 flight hours, while during the Basic Phase II training, they log six sorties with ten more flying hours. At the same time, they also log tens of flying hours with flight simulators. After graduation, students who have qualified to become fighter pilots continue their training on advanced jet trainers in 362 MEA 'Nestor' and 363 MEA 'Danaos'.

A line-up of T-37B training aircraft at Kalamata Air Base in 1978. (Hellenic Air Force)

88079/TE-079 is one of the last airworthy T-37Bs photographed on 21 February 2002 before retirement at Kalamata Air Base. (Hellenic Air Force)

032 is a T-6A Texan II armed with gun pods to perform combat patrols over Athens during the Olympic Games in 2004. (Hellenic Air Force)

023 is one of four T-6A Texan IIs often used by the T-6 display team. It is seen during landing at Larissa Air Base in May 2017. (Babak Taghvaee)

002 in front and 042 behind are T-6A Texan IIs at Kalamata Air Base in December 2022. (Axilleas Skordofoutsoglou)

021 is a T-6A Texan II seen during landing at Kalamata Air Base in December 2022. (Axilleas Skordofoutsoglou)

This specially configured T-6A Texan II of Daedalus display team at an air show in Greece in 2022. (Axilleas Skordofoutsoglou)

The jet trainers of Kalamata: T-2C/E Buckeye and M-346 training aircraft

Between 1951 and 1977, HAF received 133 Lockheed T-33A Shooting Stars and its Canadian variants from the United States, Canada, Germany and the Netherlands. These aircraft were used for a variety of missions such as pilot training, liaison and target towing, until 2000 when their last examples were retired from service.

361 Flight Training Squadron, which was established as a part of 112 PM at Elefsis Air Base, was one of the squadrons that operated T-33As for pilot training. The squadron became part of 114 PM at Tanagra in 1962 and then 111 PM in Nea Anchialos in 1963. It returned to Elefsis in 1965 still a part of 112 PM until 1970 when it moved to Kalamata, where it remains today as a part of 120 Flight Training Wing.

In 1974, the 362 MEA was renamed 362 Advanced Training Squadron and two years later it began replacing its ageing T-33As with T-2E Buckeye. In March 2006, the squadron was renamed 362 Flight Training Squadron. In addition to 362 MEA 'Nestor', 363 Operational Training Squadron (MEE) 'Danaos' was equipped with North American Rockwell T-2E Buckeyes from 9 May 1977 and was assigned to the 120 Training Wing in Kalamata. This squadron was re-designated as 363 MEA in March 2006.

'Danaos' Squadron was established on 8 January 1972 as 361 Flight Training Squadron at Larissa Air Base. Its mission was the operational training of the fourth-year cadets with F-84F Thunderflash fighter-bombers. However, the squadron also operated a large number of T-33 Mk.IIIs and later T-33As for conversion training before students flew F-84Fs. In September 1974, 361 MEA was re-designated as 363 MEE and continued its missions with just T-33As until 30 April 1977.

The contract to procure 40 T-2Es was finalized in 1975, and the aircraft were delivered in 1976 and 1977. They were delivered to 'Nestor' and 'Danaos' squadrons. Seven were lost between 1977 and 2018 and four pilots were killed. They were 160078 (unknown date), 160073 (on 8 July 1977 when pilot Theodoros Nisiotakis died), 160065 (on 25 November 1980), 160094 (on 28 July 1983 in which pilot Dionysios Panagopoulos died), 160085 (on 24 June 1996 in which pilots Georgios Roniotis and Eleftherios Tsotras died), 160098 (on 3 January 2018)' and 160097 (on 28 August 2018).

As it became more difficult to source spare parts for the T-2Es and as the number of the aircraft in service reduced, ten T-2Cs which were the unarmed variant of T-2E were procured in 1998 with delivery taking place in 2001 and 2002. Five of these ex-US Navy aircraft were cannibalized for parts while five were overhauled and put into service with 362 and 363 MEAs.

Those cadets who were selected to become fighter pilots after completing their training on T-6A Texan IIs at 361 and 364 MEAs passed their training on T-2C/Es in 362 and 363 MEAs. These two squadrons used the T-2s to train student pilots, to advanced and operational stages. During the advanced stage, the cadets learn basic fighter manoeuvring skills, navigation flight skills, instrument and formations flights, while during the operational stage, they develop their knowledge base, tactical thinking and behaviour. In this stage, they learn the use of air-to-ground weapons such as machine guns, unguided rockets and bombs since the T-2E may carry 3,500lb of ordnance under six pylons. In total, students perform 75 training sorties on T-2Es over five months.

In 2005, HAF reformed its pilot training and as a result it was planned to retire the ageing T-2C/E Buckeye with a new training jet. However, the Greek economic crisis between 2009 and 2018 delayed that process. In the years between 2005 and 2008, HAF studied and evaluated various advanced training jets such as the American Boeing T-45 Goshawk and Italian Aermacchi M-346.

Finally, a decision was made to model the future fighter pilot training centre on the Flight Academy of the Israeli Air Force. On 5 January 2021, Elbit Systems Ltd was contracted to establish this fighter pilot training centre in Kalamata under a US$1.68 billion (approximately €1.375 billion) deal to train future fighter pilots over 20 years.

To replace the ageing T-2C/Es, Elbit Systems subcontracted Leonardo to supply ten M-346 advanced jet trainers in 2021. A year after finalization of the deal, the first M-346 of the Hellenic Air Force flew to Venegono airport. The first batch of the aircraft was scheduled for delivery to 362 MEA in April 2023 allowing retirement of the last six operational T-2s (one T-2C and five T-2Es).

133 Lockheed T-33A Shooting Star and Canadair CT-133 Silver Star training jets were delivered under military aid programmes between 1951 and 1978. They were primarily used for pilot training until HAF received the T-2E Buckeye jet trainers. 61592/TR-592 was one of them. (Hellenic Air Force)

160084, a T-2E, armed with rocket pods during an exhibition at Kalamata Air Base in the early 1980s. (Hellenic Air Force)

160059 (back) and 160096 (front) are operational T-2Es photographed at the 120th Air Training Wing in December 2022. (Axilleas Skordofoutsoglou)

Three T-2Es of 120 Training Wing are taxiing towards their ramp following formation flight training in December 2022. (Axilleas Skordofoutsoglou)

160084 was one of the last six airworthy T-2E Buckeyes, which were retired in 2023. (Axilleas Skordofoutsoglou)

Training Aircraft

160084 received a special colour scheme on the 40th anniversary of delivery of T-2Es to the HAF in 2012. (Axilleas Skordofoutsoglou)

The 21 retired and four airworthy T-2C/Es at Kalamata Air Base, in December 2022, just a few months before delivery of the first M-346s and the retirement of the last T-2C/Es from service. (Axilleas Skordofoutsoglou)

Chapter 5
The Helicopters

Guardian angels of Phaethon: Agusta Bell AB.205 SAR helicopters

The Hellenic Air Force operates 16 Agusta Bell AB205A/A-1 helicopters, which are in service with 358 'Phaethon' Search and Rescue Squadron (MED) at Elefsis Air Base. These helicopters, despite being almost 50 years old, operate alongside 12 Aerospatiale AS332C1 Super Puma helicopters in service with 384 MED and play an important role in search and rescue operations across Greece particularly from the Greek Islands of the Aegean and Mediterranean seas.

The squadron also has four Bell 212s, delivered between 1976 and 1978 and have gradually replaced Agusta Bell AB206A Jet Ranger helicopters. The squadron always has two Bell 212s operational simultaneously ready to transport the Greek Prime Minister, President and other government officials. They are supplemented by another Bell 212 with VIP cabin configuration, which belongs to Hellenic Army Aviation.

From UH-19D to AB205A

In 1958, the Hellenic Air Force received four Sikorsky UH-19D Chickasaw helicopters with serial numbers 56-4274 to 4277 previously used by the US Army. These helicopters were used to form the 357 Helicopter Unit at Elefsis Air Base with a mission to undertake search and rescue missions particularly pilots of downed HAF fighter jets. In 1967, HAF received ten ex-USAF UH-19Bs, which were also based in Elefsis. With these, the 357 Helicopter unit was upgraded to squadron level.

Two years later, the 357 Helicopter Squadron became part of the 359 Civil Aviation Service Unit (359 MAEDY) based in Dekelia Air Base in Tatoi. HAF continued operating UH-19B/Ds until 1971 when the first batch of Agusta Bell AB205As were delivered. Equipped with one Lycoming T53-L-11 turboshaft engine producing 1,100shp (820kW) power, it was significantly more powerful than the ageing UH-19B/Ds, which were equipped with a Wright R-1300-3 radial piston engine producing 700shp.

In 1971, the squadron received 14 AB205As including nine from the Hellenic Army as a replacement for its ageing UH-19s. Later, in 1976, six AB205A-1s ordered specifically for the air force were delivered to the squadron. AB205A-1 was equipped with a tail rotor with longer blades on the right (starboard) side unlike the AB205 and AB205A with a small tail rotor in the left (portside). Thanks to the larger tail rotor, it was more stable and easier to control while hovering, especially when the winch operation was being performed during an SAR mission.

359 MAEDY also incorporated 352 VIP Transport Squadron, which had four Agusta Bell AB206A Jet Ranger helicopters with serial numbers 70-8620, 70-8621, 70-8627 and 70-8628. These helicopters were used to transport Greek government officials as a replacement for ageing Bell 47s. Later, the VIP helicopter fleet was reinforced with two Bell 212s, with serial numbers 30-763 and 30-765, in 1976. Two more Bell 212s with VIP cabin configuration joined the squadron in 1981. They were 31-190 and 31-196.

In November 1981, the air force received five Agusta Boeing Vertol CH-47C Chinook helicopters, which were built for Iranian Army Aviation but remained undelivered, in Italy. These helicopters entered service with 357 Helicopter Squadron to be used for personnel and materiel transportation between the Greek islands. They received serial numbers 002, 004, 006, 008 and 010. One of them crashed on 25 May 1984 and the other four were transferred to Hellenic Army Aviation in 1988.

In 1983, 358 Regular Squadron was formed in Dekelia Air Base and all helicopters in service with 352 VIP Transport Squadron and 357 Helicopter Squadron became part of the new squadron. At this point the squadron had 14 AB205As, six AB205A-1s, four AB206As, four Bell 212s and five CH-47Cs. On 10 December 1984, the squadron became a part of 112th Combat Wing and moved to Elefsis Air Base.

CH-47C with serial number 006, was lost in a non-fatal incident on 25 May 1984, and an AB205A-1 was lost in an accident on 26 July 1987. The helicopter with serial number 70-4510 crashed off Samos, in the Aegean Sea, during a medical evacuation mission during which nine occupants including three crew lost their lives. The crew were Colonel Emanuel Vasilakis (pilot), Captain Petros Panagiotakos (co-pilot) and Crew chief Warrant Officer Evangelos Valaris. They were carrying several patients and their relatives from the Amorgos and Samos Islands to 401 Army General Hospital in Athens.

In service with 358 Search and Rescue Squadron

On 18 April 1989, 359 Regular Squadron was renamed as 358 Search and Rescue Squadron (MED). Despite operating four Bell 212s and four AB206As with VIP cabin configuration, the squadron, now with 14 AB205As and five AB205A-1s in its service, had its mission focused on search and rescue (SAR), all over Greece by deploying SAR helicopters to various air bases and civil airports.

Soon after its formation, 358 MED lost two of its helicopters, on 10 May 1989 and 1 February 1990. They were AB205A with serial number 4440, and AB205A-1 with 70-4507 serial number respectively. The crash of 4440 was fatal resulting in the death of its pilot Captain Andronikos Gepis and Warrant Officer Agathoklis Golias. The helicopter crashed into Lake Pamvotida after it collided with electric wires. Only the co-pilot survived. Unlike 4440, the loss of 70-4507 was non fatal. The helicopter crashed at Lourdas Harbour.

On 20 March 2013, an Agusta Bell AB205A-1 with serial number 4511 crashed during a training flight at Viotia. The student pilot hit the ground with a tail rotor during a training flight and as a result the tail boom broke and the helicopter overturned. The student pilot was injured and survived. The aircraft was withdrawn from service and its wreckage put into storage.

Despite its age, the 358 MED has continued operating AB205s for SAR missions for five decades. As of January 2023, out of the 13 AB205As and three AB205A-1s in service, nine helicopters had been kept operational simultaneously, while three were in long-term storage and three were under maintenance.

358 MED usually has one or two AB205s at its home, Elefsis Air Base, mainly for pilot-training purposes, while seven are always on deployment across Greece. Araxos, Kalamata and Nea Anchialos air bases each have an AB205 for SAR while four others are often on deployment at civil airports including Preveza, Crete (Heraklion), Corfu and Kefalonia. They support military forces in SAR and MEDEVAC missions and are always available to rescue civilians in need.

The 358 MED continues operating the four Bell 212s for VIP flights. Two of them are kept operational while one is under maintenance and one is in storage. Since 2011, when the last operational AB206A was retired, these four Bell 212s alongside the sole Bell 212 of Hellenic Army Aviation have been the VIP helicopters in use by Greek government officials. Despite their age, they have extremely low flying hours.

The Bell 212s in service with 358 MED are available for MEDEVAC when there not needed for VIP transportation. The VIP seats inside the cabin are simply removed to provide space for loading two stretchers.

The 16 AB205s and four Bell 212s are not the only helicopters of the Hellenic Air Force. The force has 12 Aerospatiale AS332C1 Super Puma CSAR helicopters in service with 384 MED; and three Agusta A109Es and two AgustaWestland AW109S medical helicopters in service with the Emergency Medical Service Unit of the same squadron at Elefsis Air Base.

275 (c/n 551162) was the second helicopter the HAF received in February 1958. Previously used by the USAF as a search and rescue (SAR) helicopter, 56-4275 continued serving in HAF's 357 Moíra elikoptéron (ME), its helicopter squadron in the same role until replaced with an Agusta Bell AB205A in 1971. (Hellenic Air Force)

HAF operated this HH-19B SAR helicopter with serial number 952 (c/n 550460) in 357 ME until it was replaced with AB205A. It is now preserved in the air force museum at Dekelia/Tatoi airfield. (Hellenic Air Force)

70-8261 was one of four Agusta Bell AB206A JetRanger Is that 358 MED operated for almost four decades for VIP flights. (Hellenic Air Force)

4511 was an AB205A-1 in the service of 358 MED; it can be seen during an exercise in April 2006. It later crashed on 20 March 2013 and its wreckage is stored in the aircraft graveyard of Elefsis Air Base. (Hellenic Air Force)

On 11 December 2007, AB205A-1 collects a rescue diver during a training mission. (Hellenic Air Force)

Helicopter 4396, an AB205A of 358 MED during a training mission on 29 August 2011. This helicopter has been in storage at Elefsis since 2016. (Hellenic Air Force)

358 MED maintains its AB205s in the helicopter hangar of 112 Combat Wing at Elefsis Air Base. (Babak Taghvaee)

AB205A, with serial number 4397, has an engine change in the helicopter maintenance hangar of 112 Combat Wing, at Elefsis, in April 2019. (Babak Taghvaee)

30-765 is one of four Bell 212s in use for VIP transport flights. (Hellenic Air Force)

This former Iranian Army Aviation's CH-47C Chinook Transport Helicopter with serial number 004 is one of five operated by 358 MED during the 1980s. (Hellenic Air Force)

Super Pumas at Elefsis: AS332C1 search and rescue helicopters

The Hellenic Air Force operates 37 helicopters, which are in service with two search and rescue squadrons. Twenty of them, comprising 16 Agusta Bell AB205A/A1s and four Bell 212s are in service with 358 Search and Rescue Squadron (MED), while the remainder, which includes three Agusta A109Es, two AgustaWestland AW109S, and 12 Aerospatiale AS332C1s are in service with 384 MED. Similar to the AB205s, the AS332C1s are in use for search and rescue and medical evacuation. These aircraft carry equipment for combat search and rescue (CSAR) during wartime.

In 1997, the Greek government ordered four AS332C1 search and rescue helicopters for the Hellenic Coast Guard. They were purchased as part of a tender by the Ministry of Shipping, for the Coast Guard. Delivery began in December 1999 with serial number 2464 being handed over to 358 MED, an operator of 13 AB205As, four AB205A-1s, four AB206As and four Bell 212s at that time. Three more helicopters with serial numbers 2509, 2519 and 2520 were delivered by June 2000. These helicopters were painted dark grey with orange lines and large 'Rescue' titles written on their fuselage.

In 2000, four more AS332C1s were ordered, this time for use in CSAR missions for a total price of US$90 million. These helicopters with serial numbers 2574, 2575, 2584 and 2589 were delivered between June 2003 and April 2004. In 2003, two more AS332C1s configured for CSAR missions were ordered and delivered with serial numbers 2618 and 2620. The CSAR Super Pumas had different equipment for their dedicated combat missions. They were painted in two-tone blue/grey Aegean camouflage colours.

As the number of personnel within 358 MED rose following the increase in Super Pumas, decisions were made to split the squadron in half and establish a new squadron to operate the new helicopters. Subsequently, 384 MED nicknamed 'Puma' was established as a subordinate of 112 Combat Wing (PM) at Elefsis Air Base on 27 February 2006 to operate the Super Pumas. In 2010, two more AS332C1s with CSAR mission systems were ordered, and delivered in 2011.

The eight AS332C1s with 384 MED dedicated to CSAR have night-vision-goggle-compatible instrument panels, provision for the installation of exhaust nozzle heat dissipaters (for reducing infrared signature), provision for the installation of machine guns behind sliding doors, armoured doors and seats for the pilot and co-pilot and are equipped with a double hoist system. The last two, delivered in 2011 have serial numbers 2780 and 2787. All of the helicopters were equipped with searchlights and FLIR systems for night operations but, these systems, similar to the exhaust heat dissipaters, are mostly not being installed on the helicopters since they increase the weight of the aircraft as well as maintenance costs.

The current fate of the Super Puma fleet

The primary missions of 384 MED are SAR and CSAR while its secondary tasks are emergency medical service (EMS), delivery of supplies to isolated areas (particularly islands and islets of the Aegean and Mediterranean seas), transportation of personnel and cargo, general missions in support of the public, and VIP flights of military and government officials. For the EMS missions, the squadron has two AgustaWestland AW109S Trekker medical helicopters, which were ordered in 2020 and delivered in 2021. They are used by the National Centre for Emergency Care (EKAB) of Greece and operated by 384 MED.

In the years between 2003 and 2014, HAF also operated three of five Agusta A109E Power medical helicopters for EKAB. Before that, EKAB operated four helicopters until SX-HDR (c/n 11060), SX-HDT (c/n 11066) and SX-HDV (c/n 11096) were lost in crashes on 17 June 2002, 14 January 2001 and 11 February 2003. Failure of the EKAB in operating these helicopters led to delivery of the remaining three with SX-HDQ (c/n 11059), SX-HDS (c/n 11063) and SX-HDU (c/n 11070) to 358 MED in 2003. With the formation of 384 MED, they were transferred to the new squadron in February 2007 and were operated until 2014 when the last one was placed in storage.

In 2021, restoration and overhaul of the three A109Es, which had been kept in storage for years, began so that they could be operated alongside the new AW109S Trekkers with serial numbers 22701 and 22704. A109E has retractable landing gears but older Aavionic systems, while AW109S has a modern cockpit and landing skids which require less maintenance and are cheaper to maintain.

As of January 2023, 384 MED has seven AS332C1s operational simultaneously. Among them, one or two AS332C1s are always kept at Elefsis Air Base while five others are on temporary deployment. One of the two AS332C1s in Elefsis is always ready for SAR and CSAR missions while the other is held in reserve and is often used for pilot training.

384 MED always has two AS332C1s in long-term storage while one is under organizational repair in the helicopter maintenance hangar at 112 Combat Wing at Elefsis Air Base. Two other helicopters are always under heavy or depot maintenance at HAI facilities in Tangara. Between 2019 and 2022, HAI Corporation restored and repaired 2519, one of the most well known AS332C1s, which was damaged due to a hard landing in 2017.

One of the AS332C1 Super Puma helicopters with a demonstration of fast-roping by Hellenic Army Special Forces during a simulation of a CSAR mission. (Hellenic Air Force)

2584 is an AS332C1 Super Puma helicopter and can be seen during training for external carriage of cargo (sling). (Hellenic Air Force)

AS332C1 of 384 MED, with serial number 2618, is in long-term storage. (Babak Taghvaee)

2520 was one of four AS332C1s originally ordered for the Hellenic Coast Guard but was delivered to HAF. It is currently in long-term storage in Elefsis Air Base. (Babak Taghvaee)

11059 is one of three Agusta A109E Power Air Ambulance Helicopters currently under restoration. (Hellenic Air Force)

One of two Agusta Westland AW109S Trekker helicopters with serial number 22704 serial during its delivery flight on 6 March 2021. (Konstantinos Sotiropoulos)

Other books you might like:

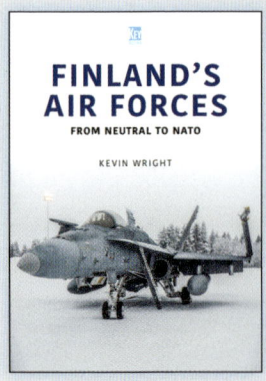
Air Forces Series, Vol. 6

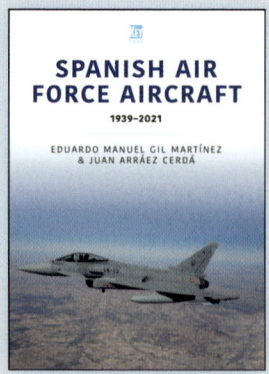
Air Forces Series, Vol. 3

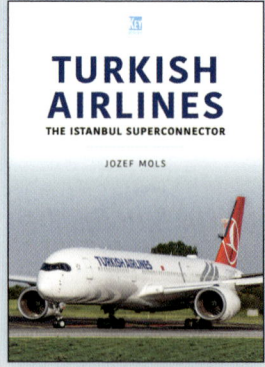
Airlines Series, Vol. 4

Airlines Series, Vol. 6

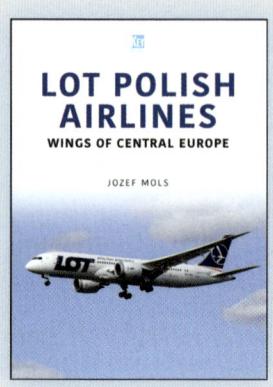
Airlines Series, Vol. 7

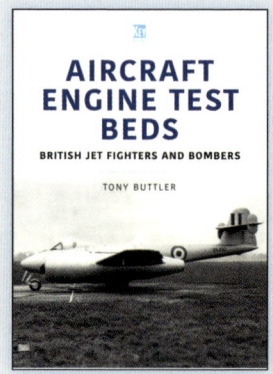

For our full range of titles please visit:
shop.keypublishing.com/books

VIP Book Club

Sign up today and receive
TWO FREE E-BOOKS

Be the first to find out about our forthcoming book releases and receive exclusive offers.

Register now at **keypublishing.com/vip-book-club**

Our VIP Book Club is a 100% spam-free zone, and we will never share your email with anyone else. You can read our full privacy policy at: privacy.keypublishing.com